Other anthologies of quotations by Gordon S. Jackson

Never Scratch a Tiger
with a Short Stick – And Other
Quotations for Leaders

Outside Insights – Quotes for
Contemporary South Africa

Quotes for the Journey,
Wisdom for the Way

Sleep Faster, We Need the Pillows –
500 Logical Lapses, Paradoxes and
Other Mental Delights

The Weather is Here, Wish You Were Beautiful –
Quotations for the Thoughtful Traveler

Watchdogs, Blogs and Wild Hogs –
A Collection of Quotations on Media

You've Made Your Bed – Now Go Bounce On It

You've Made Your Bed – Now Go Bounce On It

800 Quotes About Children, Their Parents and Others Who Care About Them

Compiled by Gordon S. Jackson

Printed in the USA by Create Space
2013

Library of Congress Control Number: 2013912948

ISBN: 1490442405
ISBN-13: 978-1490442402

Cover design by Sarah E. Jackson
Page design by Tamara Hartman Burkhead

DEDICATION

To all the children – past, present and future –
whose lives are richer, or will be, because of the
Vanessa Behan Crisis Nursery, in Spokane, Washington

ACKNOWLEDGEMENTS
AND SOURCES

This collection of quotations is indebted to the help of several individuals. They include Amy Knapton and Dina Patrick at the Vanessa Behan Crisis Nursery, who made some rich materials available to me.

A special thanks is due to Gail Fielding, in Whitworth University's library. For the last time before her retirement, she once again procured useful resources on inter-library loan. Denise Han, a Whitworth student, gave invaluable help in preparing the index.

My wife, Sue, made various comments that helped me to refine the manuscript – as did my daughter, Sarah, who also designed the book's cover; my son, Matthew; and a woman named Alice.

But the greatest debt goes to those writers and speakers who made this volume possible. Without their insights, reflections and wit, this book would not exist.

Great care has been taken in the selection of the quotations that follow to honor the fair use doctrine in copyright law. If any inadvertent omissions have occurred in this regard, these will be addressed in possible future editions of this book.

This book has drawn upon literally hundreds of sources. Occasional quotations from the Internet have been used, but the anthology is based almost entirely on authoritative print sources. Among them are:

- *A Word from the Wise,* Rosemary Jarski
- *American Heritage Dictionary of American Quotations*
- *American Quotations,* Gorton Carruth and Eugene Ehrlich
- *The Bible*

- *Camp's Unfamiliar Quotations,* Wesley D. Camp
- *Cassell's Book of Humorous Quotations*
- *Chambers Dictionary of Quotations*
- *The Children's God,* David Heller
- *The Complete Idiot's Guide to Parenting*
- *The Concise Columbia Dictionary of Quotations,* Robert Andrews
- *Dictionary of American Proverbs,* Wolfgang Mieder
- *Dictionary of Foreign Quotations,* Robert Collison
- *The Doubleday Christian Quotation Collection*
- *The Educator's Quotebook,* Edgar Dale
- *En Carta Dictionary of Quotations*
- *Family Wisdom,* Susan Ginsberg
- *The Fitzhenry and Whiteside Book of Quotations,* Robert I. Fitzhenry
- *The Funniest Thing You Never Said,* Rosemary Jarski
- *The Happiest Baby on the Block*
- *Home Book of Proverbs, Maxims and Familiar Phrases*
- *If Ignorance is Bliss, Why Aren't There More Happy People?* John Lloyd and John Mitchinson
- *Inspirational Notes, Quotes and Anecdotes that Honor Teachers and Teaching,* Robert D. Ramsey
- *The International Thesaurus of Quotations,* Rhoda Tripp
- *Leo Rosten's Carnival of Wit*
- *Life's Little Instruction Book,* H. Jackson Brown
- *The Multicultural Dictionary of Proverbs,* Harold V. Cordry
- *My soul looks back,'less I forget: a collection of quotations by people of color*
- *The New Dictionary of Thoughts*

- *The New Penguin Dictionary of Modern Quotations*
- *The New York Public Library Book of Twentieth Century American Quotations*
- *Origins: African Wisdom for Every Day*, Danielle and Olivier Föllmi
- *The Oxford Book of Aphorisms*, John Gross
- *The Oxford Dictionary of Humorous Quotations*
- *The Oxford Dictionary of Modern Quotations*
- *The Oxford Dictionary of Thematic Quotations*
- *Oxymoronica*, Mardy Grothe
- *The Pan Dictionary of Famous Quotations*
- *Parenting for Dummies*
- *The Penguin Dictionary of Modern Humorous Quotations*
- *Proverbs from Around the World*
- *The Quotable Quotations Book*, Alec Lewis
- *Quotations by Women*, Rosalie Maggio
- *Quotations for Our Time*, also published as *Peter's Quotations*, Laurence Peter
- *Simpson's Contemporary Quotations*, James B. Simpson
- *Take Time to Play Checkers*, Misti Snow
- *Toujours Tingo – More Extraordinary Words to Change the Way We See the World*, Adam Jacot de Boinod
- *A Treasury of Christian Wisdom*, Tony Castle
- *The Viking Book of Aphorisms*, W. H. Auden and Louis Kronenberger
- *What the Dormouse Said*, Amy Gish
- *Who Said What*
- *The Whole World Book of Quotations*
- *Worth Repeating*, Bob Kelly
- *21st Century Dictionary of Quotations*

"You've Made Your Bed – Now Go Bounce On It"

INTRODUCTION

Whether we think of our own children, other children we know, or even the memories of our own beginnings, "child" and "childhood" are concepts soaked in meaning and richness. We think of the potential and promise that each newborn brings to the human race. We think of their vulnerability and utter dependence on those who parent, care for and teach them. And we think too of the relentless demands that these young people make of us.

For children constitute in all our lives a mysterious common denominator. We have this impossible-to-describe bond with newborns, toddlers and even older children, regardless of language and cultural barriers. This bond no doubt arises partly from our common humanity. What is it that stirs the wonderment we share in the arrival of a newborn? This mystery of new life and its indescribable potential carries forward through infancy and childhood until we gradually tend to take people for granted as they grow into adulthood. If we think about it, the marvel of each life remains, but in reality it's the "newness" of an infant that most powerfully reminds us that life and humankind continue. As poet Carl Sandburg put it, "A baby is God's opinion that the world should go on."

So even if it's a squirming toddler sitting next to you in a lounge at O'Hare airport or a high-energy five-year-old engaging in a battle of wills with mom at the checkout counter at your grocery store, for some reason our hearts make a connection with these little persons. Why? One reason is the deep-seated recognition that "I too was once like that – once, I too needed 24-hour care and love and discipline." We can look at a child we've never seen before and say, "I can relate – I know what you're going through; I've been there. Welcome to our common membership in the human race."

As adults we are especially aware of each child's vulnerability and dependence on others for survival and nurture – and hence our individual and collective duty to care for the children in our lives and our communities. Clichéd though it is, the adage is correct: It does take a village to raise a child. At times, and for various reasons, we the "villagers" fail in our duty. We're all too aware that childhoods in many nations are lived in poverty and with chronic hunger. Or children are orphaned by AIDS, uprooted as refugees, or victims of parental neglect or even abuse. And it is also true, as Sobonfu Somé has written, that "It takes a whole village to keep parents sane."

It is this collective task of raising children and meeting their needs that provides the rationale for this book: to encourage, equip and inspire those of us whose lives overlap with those of children. Although not intended as a guide to parenting or working with children, the volume contains many quotes that speak to those needs. Mostly, though, this volume is intended simply to stretch your thinking about children and how we interact with them – as parents, grandparents or other relatives, as teachers or caregivers, or simply as other adults.

The quotes cover a wide range of children-related topics: their beginnings, their unique qualities, childhood, their learning and their play, their needs and potential, their vulnerabilities. Quotes on other topics deal with those who most profoundly affect their lives and development: fathers, mothers and parents generally.

Where do the quotes come from? Besides my own quotes on children and parenting that I have collected over the years, I have scoured both scholarly and popular literature in this area, as well as scores of other anthologies of quotations. This compilation is therefore indebted to the insights and observations of hundreds of other writers and thinkers over the ages. Some of the quotes will be familiar; most will not. But all have been selected for their potential to remind you of important ideas, introduce you to new thoughts and perspectives, or in some other way keep piquing your interest in what others have said about children and how the rest of us shape their experience of this world. The book therefore lends itself to general reading, pick-up-and-put-down browsing, or even as a reference tool.

In selecting the quotes for this anthology I have followed two principles, regarding tone and scope. First, I have striven to include quotes that reflect a realistic yet positive view of children. Societies of all kinds have throughout history typically regarded children as an inestimable gift entrusted to the care of the community. Yes, any of us who have been on a trans-Atlantic flight next to a willful toddler, or needed to calm our own infant who has been crying for hours, know that being around children is sometimes far from easy. Ask any parent, teacher or childcare provider. But this volume has for the most part resisted the temptation to include the critical, sarcastic, or other negative comments which dwell on the fact that being with kids can be difficult, exhausting or even infuriating work. Children have enough battles to deal with as they negotiate their way through life without the rest of us arming ourselves with these negative witticisms or wisecracks. Instead, children – and those of us who touch their lives – all need whatever help and encouragement we can get. I hope the tone of this book reflects that need.

The second decision was to include only quotes that pertain to pre-teen children. This was to give the book a sharper, clearer emphasis. Including entries on those young people who are bridging the years between childhood and adulthood would, I fear, have diluted the intent of this anthology. By no means is this an indication that teens are somehow less worthy of our attention; of course not. But as the line had to be drawn somewhere (aren't young adults also equally deserving of our attention?), I've chosen to focus only on those we primarily think of as children – and to exclude those who've entered that "not-quite-children, not-quite-adults" stage of the teen years.

Although this anthology is not intended as a scholarly work, I have put a high premium on accuracy and tried to obtain the most authoritative version of those quotes that circulate in more than one version. Likewise, where a quote is attributed to more than one individual, I have gone with the source that appears most authentic. I also have tried to include quotes from a wide range of national and cultural perspectives. Relatively few quotations come from non-western speakers or writers. The reason is not that U.S. and British sources are the only ones qualified to speak on this topic; far from it. It is simply that written quotes from non-western, and non-English, sources are harder to find.

Then there is the issue of inclusive language. Some quotes use "man," "mankind" and so on when referring to people in general. These quotes reflect earlier usage which characterizes contemporary English less and less. In keeping with the volume's commitment to presenting the quotes as accurately as possible, I have included these entries with their original wording.

Someone once said, "A hundred years from now it will not matter what my bank account was, the sort of house I lived in, or the kind of car I drove... But the world may be different because I was important in the life of a child." However you use this volume, for general reading, browsing or as a reference tool, I hope that these quotes will better equip, enthuse or inspire you to play that role of indispensible importance.

TOPICS

BEGINNINGS

O Creator, who does all human beings make, thou
hast a great worth on us conferred by bringing us
this little child.

– African prayer

Father asked us what was God's noblest work. Anna
said *man*, but I said *babies*. Men are often bad;
babies never are.

– Louisa May Alcott

The art of being a parent consists of sleeping when
the baby isn't looking.

– American proverb

The hot, moist smell of babies fresh from naps.

– Barbara Lazear Ascher

When the first baby laughed for the first time,
the laugh broke into a thousand pieces and they
all went skipping about, and that was the beginning
of fairies.

– James M. Barrie

Most of us would do more for our babies than
we have ever been willing to do for anyone,
even ourselves.

— Polly Berrien Berends

Babies are a nuisance, of course. But so does
everything seem to be that is worthwhile –
husbands and books and committees and being
loved and everything. We have to choose between
ease and rich unrest.

— Vera Brittain

Except that right side up is best, there is not much
to learn about holding a baby.

— Heywood Broun

People who say they sleep like a baby usually don't
have one.

— Leo J. Burke

Beware of posing as a profound person; God came
as a baby.

— Oswald Chambers

Nothing feels better than cuddling a baby.

— Debra Coppernoll

If men had to have babies they would only ever
have one each.

— Lady Diana, Princess of Wales

Every baby born into the world is a finer one than
the last.

> – Charles Dickens

Infancy conforms to nobody; all conform to it.

> – Ralph Waldo Emerson

A baby is an angel whose wings decrease as
his legs increase.

> – French proverb

Babies are such a nice way to start people.

> – Don Herold

The baby, assailed by eyes, ears, nose, skin and
intestines at once, feels it all as one great blooming,
buzzing confusion.

> – William James

The sound of a crying baby is just about the most
disturbing, shattering noise we can hear. In the
baby's crying there is no future or past, only now.
There is no appeasement, no negotiations possible,
no reasonableness.

> – Sheila Kitzinger

Baby: A loud noise at one end and no sense of
responsibility at the other.

> – Ronald Knox

Having a baby is like suddenly getting the world's worst roommate, like having Janis Joplin with a bad hangover and PMS come to stay with you.

– Annie Lamott

I just can't get over how much babies cry. I really had no idea what I was getting into. To tell you the truth, I thought it would be more like getting a cat.

– Annie Lamott

With the first-born child it is like moving into a moonless night, on an unfamiliar terrain with only a pen-light for illumination.

– Patrick Lekota

We all of us wanted babies – but did we want children?

– Eda J. LeShan

In point of fact, we are all born rude. No infant has ever appeared yet with the grace to understand how inconsiderate it is to disturb others in the middle of the night.

– Judith Martin ("Miss Manners")

It is customary to declare all babies adorable; that is the tribute we pay to the future. One of those babies will grow up to be your gerontologist.

– Judith Martin ("Miss Manners")

The whole world has changed around us in terms of workforce requirements, mothers and fathers in the workforce, divorce, and family makeup. The whole sort of social and economic fabric has changed dramatically . . . but the needs of babies haven't.
— Matthew Melmed

Of all the joys that lighten suffering earth, what joy is welcomed like a newborn child?
— Dorothy L. Nolte

Babies are always more trouble than you thought – and more wonderful.
— Charles Osgood

A baby has a way of making a man out of his father and a boy out of his grandfather.
— Angie Papadakis

Peter's Miracle Principle: Two tiny demi-chromosomed pre-protozoan flecks of amino acids unite and develop into the awesome complexity of a human being.
— Laurence Peter

There were no great men born in my home town, just babies.
— Laurence Peter

My child looked at me and I looked back at him in the delivery room and I realized that out of a sea of infinite possibilities it had come down to this: a specific person, born on the hottest day of the year, conceived on a Christmas Eve, made by his father and me miraculously from scratch.

– Anna Quindlen

A baby is God's opinion that the world should go on.

– Carl Sandburg

When I hear a baby's cry of pain change into a normal cry of hunger, to my ears that is the most beautiful music – and there are those who say I have good ears for music.

– Albert Schweitzer

Mewling, puking babies. That's the way we all start.

– Jean Shepherd

You can sort of be married, you can sort of be divorced, you can sort of be living together, but you can't sort of have a baby.

– David Shire

All some people need to make them happy is a warm bath, warm food, and a dry bottom.

– Sign at a truck stop

Birth is the arrival of somebody from another place: the person who is arriving must be welcomed, must be made to feel that she has arrived in a place where there are human beings who will receive her gifts.

– Sobonfu Somé

"Where do I come from? Where did you find me?" asks the baby of his mother. She weeps and laughs at the same time and, pressing the infant to her breasts, answers, You were hidden in my heart, darling, you were its desire.

– Rabindranath Tagore

Baby: A perfect example of minority rule.

– Unknown

The nicest thing about being a baby is that everything you do is wonderful.

– Unknown

Begin, baby boy, to recognize your mother with a smile.

– Virgil

Every child born into the world is a new thought of God, an ever-fresh and radiant possibility.

– Kate Douglas Wiggin

BLESSINGS

Children are the reward of life.

– African proverb

Sons are a gift from the Lord and children a reward from him.

– *The Bible*, Psalm 127:3 (Revised English Bible)

Few things are more rewarding than a child's uncalculating devotion.

– Vera Brittain

I love these little people; and it is not a slight thing, when they, who are so fresh from God, love us.

– Charles Dickens

The soul is healed by being with children.

– Fyodor Dostoevsky

When cares overwhelm you, take your son on your lap.

– Egyptian proverb

We find delight in the beauty and happiness of
children that makes the heart too big for the body.

– Ralph Waldo Emerson

Children are poor men's riches.

– English proverb

Happy is he who is happy in his children.

– English proverb

What a difference it makes to come home
to a child!

– Margaret Fuller

What feeling is so nice as a child's hand in yours?
So small, so soft and warm, like a kitten huddling in
the shelter of your clasp.

– Marjorie Holmes

BLESSINGS

God sends children for another purpose than
merely to keep up the race – to enlarge our hearts;
and to make us unselfish and full of kindly
sympathies and affections; to give our souls higher
aims; to call out all our faculties to extended
enterprise and exertion; and to bring round our
firesides bright faces, happy smiles, and loving,
tender hearts. My soul blesses the great Father,
every day, that he has gladdened the earth with
little children.

– Mary Howitt

One laugh of a child will make the holiest day more sacred still.

– Robert G. Ingersoll

Bricks and mortar make a house but the laughter of children make a home.

– Irish proverb

I've never outgrown that feeling of mild pride, of acceptance, when children take your hand.

– Ian McEwan

Looking after children is one way of looking after yourself.

– Ian McEwan

We don't ask people how many children they have. It is not done. Children are not goats or sheep or yams to be counted.

– Flora Nwapa, Nigerian novelist

Who has no children does not know what love is.

– Petrarch

Give a little love to a child and you will get a great deal back.

– John Ruskin

Call not that man wretched, who, whatever ills he suffers, has a child to love.

– Robert Southey

How can there be too many children? That is like saying there are too many flowers.

– Mother Teresa

What a blessing a child is in our old age!

– Theaetetus Scholasticus

A child is like a dugout canoe. If you make one, it will one day get you across water.

– Warega oral tradition (Africa)

BOYS AND GIRLS, SONS AND DAUGHTERS

A girl is Innocence playing in the mud,
Beauty standing on its head, and
Motherhood dragging a doll by the foot.

– Allen Beck

Little girls are the nicest things that happen
to people.

– Allan Beck

A trick that everyone abhors
In little girls is slamming doors.

– Hillaire Belloc

Boy: Someone who wants to grow up fast and be
a fireman and eat candy for a living.

– Eugene E. Brussell

Oh my son's my son till he gets him a wife,
But my daughter's my daughter all her life.
                              – Dinah Mulock Craik

What are little boys made of?
Frogs and snails
And puppy-dogs; tails.
That's what little boys are made of.
                              – English nursery rhyme

What are little girls made of?
Sugar and spice
And all that's nice,
That's what little girls are made of.
                              – English nursery rhyme

One boy is more trouble than a dozen girls.
                              – English proverb

When I grow up I want to be a little boy.
                              – Joseph Heller

Be patient with the boys – you are dealing with soul
stuff. Destiny awaits just around the corner.
                              – Elbert Hubbard

A man who has only sons and who has never
fathered a daughter has lost a little bit of heaven
on earth.
                              – Irish proverb

Kaplan's Law of the Instrument: Give a small boy
a hammer and he will find that everything he
encounters needs pounding.

– Abraham Kaplan

There was a little girl
Who had a little curl
Right in the middle of her forehead;
When she was good
She was very, very good,
But when she was bad she was horrid.

– Henry Wadsworth Longfellow

Boys are found everywhere – on top of,
underneath, inside of, climbing on, swinging
from, running around or jumping to. Mothers
love them, little girls hate them, older sisters
and brothers tolerate them, adults ignore them
and heaven protects them.

– New England Life Insurance Company pamphlet,
"What is a boy?" (1956)

Little girls are the nicest things that happen to
people. They are born with a little bit of angel-shine
about them, and although it wears thin sometimes
there is always enough left to lasso your heart –
even when they are sitting in the mud, or crying
temperamental tears, or parading up the street in
mother's best clothes.

– New England Life Insurance Company pamphlet,
"What is a girl?" (1956)

Of all the animals, the boy is the
most unmanageable.

– Plato

You don't raise heroes, you raise sons. And if you
treat them like sons, they'll turn out to be heroes,
even if it's just in your own eyes.

– Walter Schirra Sr.

A boy is a noise with some dirt on it.

– Unknown

A daughter is mystery and enchantment and magic
and fantasy all rolled up in a small strange package.

– Dan Valentine

One of the best things in the world to be is a boy; it
requires no experience but needs some practice to
be a good one.

– Charles Dudley Warner

BOYS AND GIRLS, SONS AND DAUGHTERS

CHILDHOOD

Backward, turn backward, O Time, in the flight;
Make me a child again, just for tonight.
– Elizabeth Akers Allen

Blessed be childhood, which brings down
something of heaven into the midst of our rough
earthliness.
– Henri Frédéric Amiel

Childhood is measured out by sounds and smells
And sights, before the dark of reason grows.
– John Betjeman

Enjoying childhood experiences to the full is the
best preparation for becoming a mature adult.
– Bruno Bettelheim

Childhood is never troubled with foresight.
– Fanny Burney

Boyhood is a most complex and incomprehensible thing. Even when one has been through it, one does not understand what it was. A man can never quite understand a boy, even when he has been the boy.

– G. K. Chesterton

A happy childhood is one of the best gifts that parents have it in their power to bestow.

– Mary Cholmondeley

One of the luckiest things that can happen to you in life is, I think, to have a happy childhood.

– Agatha Christie

The illusions of childhood are necessary experiences: a child should not be denied a balloon just because an adult knows that sooner or later it will burst.

– Marcelene Cox

For me, the greatest tragedy of life is that childhood is such a short part of our lives.

– Henry Dormann

We see these adolescents mourning for a lost childhood.

– David Elkind, Professor of Child Study, on children pushed into sports, music or academics

Childhood is a short season.

– Helen Hayes

The primary need of children is not better laws or public programs. It is better childhoods.

– Jack Kemp

Childhood is freedom.

– Kashmiri proverb

I suppose we all tend to remember only the happiness from our childhood, as a sundial refuses to tell the time except in fine weather.

– Bernard Levin

Childhood is the Kingdom Where Nobody Dies. Nobody that matters, that is.

– Edna St. Vincent Millay

Childhood shows the man, as morning shows the day.

– John Milton

The greatest poem ever known
Is one all poets have outgrown:
The poetry, innate, untold,
Of being only four years old.

– Christopher Morley

I remember, I remember
How my childhood fleeted by –
The mirth of its December
And the warmth of its July.

– Winthrop Praed

What one loves in childhood stays in the
heart forever.

– Mary Jo Putney

Hold childhood in reverence and do not be in any
hurry to judge it for good or ill. Give nature time
to work before you take over her tasks, lest you
interfere with her method.

– Jean Jacques Rousseau

A child's business is an open yard, into which any
passer-by may peer curiously. It is no house, not
even a glass house. A child's reticence is a little
white fence around her business, with a swinging,
helpless gate through which grown-ups come in or
go out, for there are no locks on your privacy.

– Margaret Lee Runbeck

I can remember, at the age of five, being told that
childhood was the happiest period of life (a blank
lie, in those days). I wept inconsolably, wished I
were dead, and wondered how I should endure the
boredom of the years to come.

– Bertrand Russell

Children without a childhood are tragic.

– Mendele Mocher Seforim

Nobody ever told me before [William Blake] did
that childhood is such a damned serious business.

– Maurice Sendak

Childhood is Last Chance Gulch for happiness.
After that, you know too much.

— Tom Stoppard

If you carry your childhood with you, you never
become older.

—Tom Stoppard

Childhood: That wonderful time when all you need
to lose weight is to bathe.

— Unknown

Childhood is frequently a solemn business for those
inside it.

— George F. Will

CHILDREN AND GROWN-UPS

Never break off communication with your children, no matter what they do.

— H. Jackson Brown

If you treat a sick child like an adult and a sick adult like a child, everything usually works out pretty well.

— Ruth Carlisle

It is not a bad thing that children should occasionally, and politely, put parents in their place.

— Sidonie-Gabrielle Colette

Children are surely one of God's greatest gifts and truest challenges. To share your life with a child is to humble yourself so that you may learn from them and discover with them the beautiful secrets that are only uncovered in searching.

— Kathleen Tierney Crilly

Women make us poets, children make us philosophers.

– Malcolm de Chazal

Grown-ups never understand anything for themselves, and it is tiresome for children to be always and forever explaining things to them.

– Antoine de Saint-Exupéry

Who of us is mature enough for offspring before the offspring themselves arrive? The value of marriage is not that adults produce children but that children produce adults.

– Peter de Vries

An adult is one who has lost the grace, the freshness, the innocence of the child, who is no longer capable of feeling pure joy, who makes everything complicated, who spreads suffering everywhere, who is afraid of being happy, and who, because it is easier to bear, has gone back to sleep. The wise man is a happy child.

– Arnaud Desjardins

Love children especially, for like the angels they too are sinless, and they live to soften and purify our hearts, and, as it were, to guide us. Woe to him who offends a child!

– Fyodor Dostoevsky

The greatest lessons in life, if we would but stoop and humble ourselves, we would learn not from the grown-up learned men, but from the so-called ignorant children.

– Mohandas Gandhi

The most sophisticated people I know – inside they are all children.

– Jim Henson

One of the most obvious facts about grown-ups to a child is that they have forgotten what it is like to be a child.

– Randall Jarrell

A great man is one who knows that he was not put on earth to be part of a process through which a child can be hurt.

– Murray Kempton

The secret of dealing successfully with a child is not to be its parent.

– Mell Lazarus

Children have one kind of silliness, as you know, and grown-ups have another kind.

– C. S. Lewis

CHILDREN AND GROWN-UPS

When you take the time to actually listen, with humility, to what people have to say, it's amazing what you can learn. Especially if the people who are doing the talking also happen to be children.

– Greg Mortenson

The art of dealing with children might be defined as *knowing what not to say*.

– A. S. Neill

[W]hat's wrong with grown-ups . . . is that they think they know all the answers.

– Zilpha Keatley Snyder

Parents learn a lot from their children about coping with life.

– Muriel Spark

Do but gain a boy's trust; convince him by your behavior that you have his happiness at heart; let him discover that you are the wiser of the two; let him experience the benefits of following your advice and the evils that arise from disregarding it; and fear not you will readily enough guide him.

– Herbert Spencer

In the United States today, there is a pervasive tendency to treat children as adults, and adults as children. The options of children are thus steadily expanded, while those of adults are progressively constricted. The result is unruly children and childish adults.

– Thomas Szasz

You don't really understand human nature unless you know why a child on a merry-go-round will wave at his parents every time around – and why the parents wave back.

– Bill Tammeus

If you want to learn something, listen to the children.

– Turkish proverb

CHILDREN AND GROWN-UPS

COMMUNITY

Since children are a group responsibility, a man may not marry and found a household before he has a hut and tillable land.

— African oral tradition

It takes a village to raise a child.

— African proverb

We should begin by ensuring that every child in the world is able to eat and go to school. Let us internationalize children, no matter where they are born, by treating them as a world heritage deserving of the entire world's attention.

— Cristovam Buarque

What the best and wisest parent wants for his own child, that must the community want for all its children.

— John Dewey

Whether or not you have children yourself, you are a parent to the next generation. If we can only stop thinking of children as individual property and think of them as the next generation, then we can realize we all have a role to play.

– Charlotte Davis Kasl

What its children become, that will the community become.

– Suzanne LaFollette

There can be no keener revelation of a society's soul than the way in which it treats its children.

– Nelson Mandela

Adorable children are considered to be the general property of the human race. (Rude children belong to their mothers.)

– Judith Martin ("Miss Manners")

We must have . . . a place where children can have a whole group of adults they can trust.

– Margaret Mead

What the world needs is not romantic lovers who are sufficient unto themselves, but husbands and wives who live in communities, relate to other people, carry on useful work and willingly give time and attention to their children.

– Margaret Mead

COMMUNITY

Two parents can't raise a child any more than one. You need a whole community – everybody – to raise a child.

– Toni Morrison

If a child grows up with the idea that Mom and Dad are her only community, then when she has a problem, if the parents cannot fix it, she doesn't have anybody else to turn to.

– Sobonfu Somé

It takes a whole village to keep parents sane.

– Sobonfu Somé

DISCIPLINE

Whenever a child lies you will always find a severe parent. A lie would have no sense unless the truth were felt to be dangerous.

– Alfred Adler

It is ominous for the future of a child when the discipline he receives is based on the emotional needs of the disciplinarian rather than on any consideration of the child's own needs.

– Gordon W. Allport

Teach your child to hold his tongue; he'll learn fast enough to speak.

– American proverb

The habits we form from childhood make no small difference, but rather they make all the difference.

– Aristotle

Don't demand respect, as a parent. Demand civility and insist on honesty. But respect is something you must earn – with kids as well as with adults.

– William Attwood

No child is ever spoiled by too much attention. It is the lack of attention that spoils.

– Bessie Blake

Loving a child doesn't mean giving in to all his whims; to love him is to bring out the best in him, to teach him to love what is difficult.

– Nadia Boulanger

My concept of a spoiled child is that of an anxious child, searching for its limits. If no one provides them, she must keep searching.

– T. Berry Brazelton

Don't allow your children or grandchildren to call you by your first name.

– H. Jackson Brown

Anger is to be specially avoided in inflicting punishment.

– Cicero

Our children are counting on us to provide two things: consistency and structure. Children need parents who say what they mean, mean what they say, and do what they say they are going to do.

– Barbara Coloroso

It is a mystery why adults expect perfection from children. Few grownups can get through a whole day without making a mistake.

– Marcelene Cox

Discipline is a symbol of caring to a child. He needs guidance. If there is love, there is no such thing as being too tough with a child . . . . If you have never been hated by your child, you have never been a parent.

– Bette Davis

Dare to Discipline

– James Dobson, book title

The parent must convince himself that discipline is not something he does to the child; it is something he does for the child.

– James Dobson

I am recommending a simple principle: When you are defiantly challenged, win decisively. When the child asks, "Who's in charge?" tell him. When he mutters, "Who loves me?" take him in your arms and surround him with affection. Treat with with respect and dignity, and expect the same from him. Then begin to enjoy the sweet benefits of competent parenthood.

– James Dobson

Thou shalt not belittle your child.

– Fitzhugh Dodson

Fences, unlike punishments, clearly mark out the perimeters of any specified territory. Young children learn where it is permissible to play, because their backyard fence plainly outlines the safe area. They learn about the invisible fence that surrounds the stove, and that Grandma has an invisible barrier around her cabinet of antique teacups.

– Jeanne and Don Elium

Any child can tell you that the sole purpose of a middle name is so he can tell when he's really in trouble.

– Dennis Frakes

If you have to yell at your kids, you're not close enough to them.

– Virgil Hardin

If from infancy you treat children as gods they are liable in adulthood to act as devils.

– P. D. James

If there is anything we wish to change in the child, we should first examine it and see whether it is not something that could be better changed in ourselves.

– Carl Jung

The real menace in dealing with a five-year-old is that in no time at all you start to sound like a five-year-old.

– Jean Kerr

Remember, when they have a tantrum, don't have one of your own.

– Judith Kuriansk

What the vast majority of American children need is to stop being pampered, stop being indulged, stop being chauffeured, stop being catered to. In the final analysis it is not what you do for your children but what you have taught them to do for themselves that will make them successful human beings.

– Ann Landers

Let your rules to your son be as few as is possible. 33

– John Locke

The first idea that the child must acquire in order to be actively disciplined is that of the difference between good and evil; and the task of the educator lies in seeing that the child does not confound good with immobility, and evil with activity.

– Maria Montessori

Call them rules or call them limits, good ones, I believe, have this in common: they serve reasonable purposes; they are practical and within a child's capability; they are consistent; and they are an expression of loving concern.

– Fred Rogers

The best time to punish is not when we are at our maddest, but that's usually when we do it.

– Nancy Samalin

The main source of good discipline is growing up in a loving family, being loved and learning to love in return.

– Benjamin Spock

Train your child in the way in which you know you should have gone yourself.

– Charles Haddon Spurgeon

With children we must mix gentleness with firmness. They must not always have their own way, but they must not always be thwarted. If we never have headaches through rebuking them, we shall have plenty of heartaches when they grow up. Be obeyed at all costs; for if you yield up your authority once, you will hardly get it again.

– Charles Haddon Spurgeon

A child should always say what's true
And speak when he is spoken to,
And behave mannerly at table;
At least as far as he is able.

– Robert Louis Stevenson

Permissiveness is the principle of treating children as if they were adults, and the tactic of making sure they never reach that stage.

– Thomas Szasz

Don't threaten a child; either punish or forgive him.

– *The Talmud*

It is better to bind your children to you by a feeling of respect, and by gentleness, than by fear.

– Terence

We are permissive until we can't stand our kids, then autocratic until we can't stand ourselves.

– Unknown

[Parents] must get across the idea that "I love you always, but sometimes I do not love your behavior."

– Amy Vanderbilt

It's funny the way a parent's raised eyebrow can do more damage to your psyche than, say, Chinese water torture.

– Arabella Weir

No one knows better than children how much they need the authority that protects, that sets the outer limits of behavior with known and prescribed consequences. As one little boy expressed it to his mother, "You care what I do."

– Leontine Young

EXAMPLE AND INFLUENCE

He helped people see God in the ordinary things of life, and he made children laugh.
> – Wilbert V. Awdry (an English clergyman who wrote the *Thomas the Tank Engine* books; this was his preferred epitaph)

Parents who wish to train up their children in the way they should go, must go in the way in which they would have their children go.
> – Francis Bacon

Children have never been very good at listening to their elders, but they have never failed to imitate them.
> – James Baldwin

The question for the child is not "Do I want to be good?" but "Whom do I want to be like?"
> – Bruno Bettelheim

Children need parents who model self-discipline rather than preach it. They learn from what their parents actually do, not from what they say they do . . . .

– John Bradshaw

Example is the school of mankind, and they will learn at no other.

– Edmund Burke

Don't worry that children never listen to you. Worry that they are always watching you.

– Robert Fulghum

Children are like wet cement. Whatever falls on them makes an impression.

– Haim Ginott

The proper time to influence the character of a child is about a hundred years before he is born.

– Dean Inge (also attributed to others)

If you are planning any misdeed, never forget that a child has a first claim on your respect.

– Juvenal

Children may forget what you say, but they'll never forget how you made them feel.

– Parker J. Palmer

EXAMPLE AND INFLUENCE

What we do to our children, they will do to society.
— Pliny the Elder

There are only three ways to teach a child: the first is by example, the second is by example, and the third is by example.
— Albert Schweitzer

Careful the tale you tell . . .
Children will listen.
— Stephen Sondheim

Most kids hear what you say; some kids do what you say; but all kids do what you do.
— Kathleen Casey Theisen

A hundred years from now it will not matter what my bank account was, the sort of house I lived in, or the kind of car I drove . . . . But the world may be different because I was important in the life of a child.
— Unknown

Be careful of your life lest a child stumble over you.
— Unknown

What children hear at home soon flies abroad.
— Unknown

A child's mind is like a bank – whatever you put in, you get back in ten years, with interest.

– Frederic Wertham

Every word and deed of a parent is a fiber woven into the character of a child, which ultimately determines how that child fits into the fabric of society.

– David Wilkerson

Give me the children until they are seven and anyone may have them afterwards.

– Francis Xavier

EXAMPLE AND INFLUENCE

FAITH

Dear God: When is the best time I can talk with you? I know you are always listening, but when will you be listening especially hard in Ann Arbor, Michigan?
— Allen (from *The Children's God* by David Heller)

The religion of a child depends on what its mother and father are, and not on what they say.
— Henri-Frédéric Amiel

The best way to teach morality is to make it a habit with children.
— Aristotle

Never force religious instruction on your child. It is far more important for him to feel the impact of your faith . . . . If your faith is really living in you, you will not need to depend on pious words: your children will sense it in your daily life and in your contact with them.
— Johann Christoph Arnold

Let the little children come to me, and do not hinder them, for the kingdom of God belongs to such as these.

– *The Bible*, Mark 10:14 (*New International Version*)

When I have a problem I go to my parents, but if I have a problem I can't tell my parents, I go to God.

– Joe, aged 12 (from *Take Time to Play Checkers* by Misti Snow)

Dear God: How do you feel about people who don't believe in you? Somebody else wants to know.

– Neil (from *The Children's God* by David Heller)

When home is ruled according to God's Word, angels might be asked to stay with us, and they would not find themselves out of their element.

– Charles Haddon Spurgeon

I'm convinced that one of the most powerful forces on earth is the prayer of a child.

– Wess Stafford

Dear God: Are boys better than girls? I know you are one [a boy], but try to be fair.

– Sylvia (from *The Children's God* by David Heller)

Dear Father of the World Family,
Please take care of all children everywhere.
Keep them safe from all danger,
And help them grow up strong and good.

– The Infant Teachers Prayer Book

Your children are the greatest gift God will give to you, and their souls the heaviest responsibility He will place in your hands. Take time with them, teach them to have faith in God. Be a person in whom they can have faith. When you are old, nothing else you've done will have mattered as much.

– Lisa Wingate

FAMILIES

The only normal families are the ones you don't know very well.

— Joe Ancis

I worry about people who get born nowadays, because they get born into such tiny families – sometimes into no family at all. When you're the only pea in the pod, your parents are likely to get you confused with the Hope Diamond.

— Russell Baker

A happy family is but an earlier heaven.

— John Bowring (also attributed to others)

In a united family, happiness springs up of itself.

— Chinese proverb

No family can hang out the sign, "Nothing the matter here."

— Chinese proverb

What families have in common around the world is that they are the place where people learn who they are and how to be that way.

— Jean Illsley Clarke

Healthy families are our greatest national resource.

— Dolores Curran

The family is the nucleus of civilization.

— Will and Ariel Durant

It is easier to rule a kingdom than to regulate a family.

— Japanese proverb

FAMILIES

As the family goes, so goes the nation and so goes the whole world in which we live.

— Pope John Paul II

The family you come from isn't as important as the family you're going to have.

— Ring Lardner

The family was ordained of God that children might be trained up for himself . . . .

— Pope Leo XIII

The first world we find ourselves in is a family that is not of our choosing.

— Harriet Lerner

No matter how many communes anybody invents,
the family always creeps back.

– Margaret Mead

A family is a unit composed not only of children,
but of men, women, an occasional animal, and the
common cold.

– Ogden Nash

The oldest of all social groups, and the only natural
one, is the family.

– Jean Jacques Rousseau

The family is one of nature's masterpieces.

– George Santayana

Bringing up a family should be an adventure,
not an anxious discipline in which everybody is
constantly graded for performance.

– Milton Sapirstein

[In a big family] the first child is kind of like the
first pancake. If it's not perfect, that's okay, there are
a lot more coming along.

– Antonin Scalia

Perhaps the greatest social service that can be
rendered by anybody to the country and to
mankind is to bring up a family.

– George Bernard Shaw

The difficulty about our family system remains:
Adults need quiet, order, and cleanliness; and
children need noise, dirt and destructiveness.

– George Bernard Shaw

A family that prays together stays together.

– Mother Teresa (also attributed to others)

[I]t is the family that gives us a deep private sense
of belonging. Here we first begin to have our self
defined for us.

– Howard Thurman

Happy families are all alike; every unhappy family
is unhappy in its own way.

– Leo Tolstoy

There is a sense in which the family is made by
the individuals who constitute it, but there is a far
deeper sense in which the individuals are made by
the family.

– Elton Trueblood

You don't choose your family. They are God's gift to
you, as you are to them.

– Desmond Tutu

The Universal Declaration of Human Rights describes the family as the natural and fundamental unit of society. It follows that any choice and decision with regard to the size of the family must irrevocably rest with the family itself and cannot be made by anyone else.

– United Nations

Loving relationships are a family's best protection against the challenges of the world.

– Bernie Weibe

FAMILIES

FATHERS
AND FATHERHOOD

No father has really tasted the thrill of fatherhood until his six-year-old daughter starts waiting on him hand and foot.

– O. A. Battista

Fathers, don't over-correct your children, or they will grow up feeling inferior and frustrated.

– *The Bible*, Colossians 3:20 (*The New Testament in Modern English*, J. B. Phillips)

My heart is happy, my mind is free – I had a father who talked with me.

– Hilda Bigelow

When I was about to become a father, my friend Burgess Meredith said, "You're gonna find something wonderful – someone you love more than yourself." For self-centered people, it's a great blessing.

– Peter Boyle

Don't be a pal to your son. Be his father. What child needs a 40-year-old for a friend?

– Al Capp

How sad that men would base an entire civilization on the principle of paternity, upon legal ownership and presumed responsibility for children, and then never really get to know their sons and daughters very well.

– Phyllis Chesler

No music is so pleasant to my ears as that word – "father."

– Lydia Maria Child

It is not a father's anger but his silence that a son dreads.

– Chinese proverb

The biggest social problem in our society may be the growing absence of fathers from their children's homes because it contributes to so many other social problems.

– Bill Clinton

Fatherhood is pretending the present you love most is soap-on-a-rope.

– Bill Cosby

A king, realizing his incompetence, can
either delegate or abdicate his duties. A father
can do neither.

– Marlene Dietrich

What a father says to his children is not heard by
the world, but it will be heard by posterity.

– Jean Paul Eixhter

He was generous with his affection, given to great,
awkward, engulfing hugs, and I can remember
so clearly the smell of his hugs, all starched shirt,
tobacco, Old Spice and Cutty Sark. Sometimes I
think I've never been properly hugged since.

– Linda Ellerbee

A father is a tower of strength to his sons.

– Euripides

There is something ultimate in a father's love,
something that cannot fail, something to be
believed against the whole world.

– Frederick W. Faber

A father is a banker provided by nature.

– French proverb

I could not point to any need in childhood as
strong as that for a father's protection.

– Sigmund Freud

My father was frightened of his mother, I was frightened of my father, and I'm damned well going to make sure that my children are frightened of me.
– King George V of England

We have arrived at a consensus that fathers have been lost and must be found.
– Ellen Goodman

One father is more than a hundred schoolmasters.
– George Herbert

The most important thing a father can do for his children is to love their mother.
– Theodore M. Hesburgh

Don't take up a man's time talking about the smartness of your children; he wants to talk about the smartness of his children.
– Ed Howe

It is easier for a father to have children than for children to have a real father.
– Pope John XXIII

Examine yourselves: ask yourselves, each of you, have I been a good . . . husband? . . . father? If not, all professions of religion will avail me nothing.
– Charles Kingsley

Like father, like son: every good tree maketh good fruits.

> – William Langland, *Piers Plowman* (14th century)

It is much easier to become a father than to be one.

> – Kent Nerburn

I know that my father loved me – but he did not seem to wish me to see it.

> – John Newton

The kind of man who thinks that helping with the dishes is beneath him will also think that helping with the baby is beneath him, and then he certainly is not going to be a very successful father.

> – Eleanor Roosevelt

A good father is a little bit of a mother.

> – Lee Salk

It is a wise father that knows his own child.

> – William Shakespeare, *The Merchant of Venice*

And what could my father possibly want with another child, when he hardly bothered to talk to the one he already had?

> – Polly Shulman

The best a father can give to his son is the gift of himself – his time. For material things mean little, if there is not someone to share them with.

– Neil C. Strait

When I was a boy of fourteen, my father was so ignorant I could hardly stand to have the old man around. But when I got to be twenty-one, I was astonished how much he had learned in seven years.

– Mark Twain

FOOD AND DRINK

Child: An appetite surrounded by noise.
– Changing Times

Every meal tastes better if you end it with a peanut butter sandwich.
– John Coppernoll

Komvya, a word in the Mambwe language, in Zambia, meaning: To feed a child with one's finger.
– Adam Jacot de Boinod, Toujours Tingo – More Extraordinary Words to Change the Way We See the World

The baby who does not cry does not get fed.
– French proverb

A growing boy has a wolf in his belly.
– German proverb

It's odd how large a part food plays in memories of childhood. There are grown men and women who still shudder at the sight of spinach, or turn away with loathing from stewed prunes and tapioca. . . . Luckily, however, it's the good taste one remembers best.

– Caroline Lejeune

It's hard to get your kids to eat food if it hasn't danced on TV first.

– Linda Mullen (also attributed to others)

I don't care how busy you are – you can take [mealtime] with your children. You can talk about your dreams; you can talk about your day; you can talk about your frustrations. The busier you are, the more valuable meal time is for your child. If we don't spend this time with our youngsters, they are not going to develop healthy attitudes toward family life.

– Lee Salk

The remarkable thing about my mother is that for thirty years she served us nothing but leftovers. The original meal has never been found.

– Calvin Trillin

There's nothing thirstier than a child who has just gone to bed.

– Unknown

A food is not necessarily essential just because your child hates it.

– Katharine Whitehorn

GRANDPARENTS

A house needs a grandma in it.

— Louisa May Alcott

The best baby-sitters, of course, are the baby's grandparents. You feel completely comfortable entrusting your baby to them for long periods, which is why most grandparents flee to Florida.

— Dave Barry

A grandfather is a man who can't understand how his idiot son had such brilliant children.

— Milton Berle

Grandparents who want to be truly helpful will do well to keep their mouths shut and their opinions to themselves until these are requested.

— T. Berry Brazelton

Because they are usually free to love and guide and befriend the young without having to take daily responsibility for them, they can often reach out past pride and fear of failure and close the space between generations.

– Jimmy Carter

Over the river and through the wood,
To Grandfather's house we go.

– Lydia Maria Child (from an 1844 poem;
a more recent version recorded as a song
refers to "Grandmother's house")

A grandmother doesn't have to do anything except be there. . . . . Grandmothers are the only grown-ups who have got time.

– Patsy Gray

What children need most are the essentials that grandparents provide in abundance. They give unconditional love, kindness, patience, humor, comfort, and lessons in life. And, most importantly, cookies.

– Rudolph Guliani

Grandparents somehow sprinkle a sense of stardust over grandchildren.

– Alex Haley

There are fathers who do not love their children; there is no grandfather who does not adore his grandson.

— Victor Hugo

A home without a grandmother is like an egg without salt.

— Florence King

No one . . . who has not known the inestimable privilege can possibly realize what good fortune it is to grow up in a home where there are grandparents.

— Suzanne LaFollette

There is nothing like having grandchildren to restore your faith in heredity.

— Doug Larson

The simplest toy, which even the youngest child can operate, is called a grandparent.

— Sam Levenson

Something magical happens when parents turn into grandparents. Their attitude changes from "money doesn't grow on trees" to spending it like it does.

— Paula Linden

The closest friends I have made through life have been people who also grew up close to a loved and loving grandmother or grandfather.

— Margaret Mead

By the time the youngest children have learned to keep the place tidy, the oldest grandchildren are on hand to tear it to pieces again.

– Christopher Morley

A grandmother is a person with too much wisdom to let that stop her from making a fool of herself over her grandchildren.

– Phil Moss

The commonest axiom of history is that every generation revolts against its fathers and makes friends with its grandfathers.

– Lewis Mumford

Have children while your parents are still young enough to take care of them.

– Rita Rudner

We have become a grandmother.

– Margaret Thatcher

One thing you can say for small children – they don't go around showing off pictures of their grandparents.

– Unknown

Never have children, only grandchildren.

– Gore Vidal

GRANDPARENTS

Grandchildren are God's way of compensating us for growing old.

– Mary H. Waldrip

Perfect love sometimes does not come until the first grandchild.

– Welsh proverb

A mother becomes a true grandmother the day she stops noticing the terrible things her children do because she is so enchanted with the wonderful things her grandchildren do.

– Lois Wyse

GROWING UP

When childhood dies, its corpses are called adults.
– Brian Aldiss

When wings are grown, birds and children fly away.
– Chinese proverb

Boys do not grow up gradually. They move forward in spurts like the hands of clocks in railway stations.
– Cyril Connolly

Let your children go if you want to keep them.
– Malcolm Forbes

A child enters your home and makes so much noise for twenty years you can hardly stand it – then departs, leaving the house so silent you think you will go mad.
– J. A. Holmes

It kills you to see them grow up. But I guess it would kill you quicker if they didn't.
– Barbara Kingsolver

Growing and learning and obeying the rules of their elders, or fighting against them, are not easy things to do.

— Don Marquis

We've had bad luck with our kids – they've all grown up.

— Christopher Morley

One stops being a child when one realizes that telling one's troubles does not make it any better.

— Cesare Pavese

First, the cradle, then the crib, the big-boy bed, the posters on the wall, the prom pictures on the desk. And then the U-Haul and the tiny kitchen with the lone pan. His home is now elsewhere.

— Anna Quindlen

Adults are obsolete children.

— Dr. Seuss (Theodore Geisel)

Our children are here to stay, but our babies and toddlers and preschoolers are gone as fast as they can grow up – and we have only a short moment with each. When you see a grandfather take a baby in his arms, you see that the moment hasn't always been long enough.

— St Clair Adams Sullivan

A child becomes an adult when he realizes he has a right not only to be right but also to be wrong.

— Thomas Szasz

It takes courage to let our children go, but we are
trustees and stewards and have to hand them back
to life, to God.

– Alfred Torrie

After you grow up, is there anything else?

– Unknown child

Train up a child in the way he should go, and
before you know it, he's gone.

– Unknown

You, my dear child,
I can teach all about AIDS, but I cannot protect
you from HIV.
I can tell you things, but I cannot be responsible
for them.
I can advise you, but I cannot decide for you.
I can talk about drink and about drugs, but I
cannot say no in your place.
I can teach you goodness, but I cannot give
you morality.
I can teach you respect, but I cannot make
you honorable.
I can pass on values, but I cannot make you moral.
I can give you love, but I cannot give you
inner beauty.
I have given you life, but I cannot do your
living for you.

– Abner Xoagub

HUMOR

Out of the mouth of babes – usually when you've got your best suit on.

– Geraldine Baxter

There are two classes of travel: first class, and with children.

– Robert Benchley

Reinhart was never his mother's favorite – and he was an only child.

– Thomas Berger

I'm going to stop punishing my children by saying, "Never mind! I'll do it myself."

– Erma Bombeck

It goes without saying that you should never have more children than you have car windows.

– Erma Bombeck

When my kids become wild and unruly, I use a nice safe playpen. When they're finished, I climb out.

– Erma Bombeck

I was toilet-trained at gunpoint.

– Billy Brever

Bachelor's wives and old maids' children are always perfect.

– Nicolas Chamfort

The thing that best defines a child is the total inability to receive information from anything not plugged in.

– Bill Cosby

When traveling with children on one's holidays, at least one child of any number of children will request a rest room stop exactly half way between any two given rest areas.

– Mervyn Cripps

Cleaning your house while your children are still growing is like shoveling the walk before it stops snowing.

– Phyllis Diller

You can learn many things from children. How much patience you have, for instance.

– Franklin P. Jones

Ask your child what he wants for dinner only if he's buying.

– Fran Lebowitz

Never allow your child to call you by your first name. He hasn't known you long enough.
– Fran Lebowitz

An unusual child is one who asks his parents questions they can answer.
– E. C. McKenzie

Prodigy: A child who plays the piano when he should be in bed.
– J. B. Morton

I take my children everywhere, but they always find their way back home.
– Robert Orben

The birth of a baby brings joy into the house: it might have been twins.
– Frank Richardson

Before I got married I had six theories about bringing up children; now I have six children and no theories.
– Lord Rochester

There are only two things a child will willingly share: communicable diseases and his mother's age.
– Benjamin Spock

An easy way not to get rich is to have plenty
of children.

– Unknown

Children come from God. He can't stand the
noise either.

– Unknown

If it was going to be easy to raise kids, it never
would have started with something called labor.

– Unknown

The main purpose of children's parties is to remind
you that there are children worse than your own.

– Katharine Whitehorn

LEARNING

Train a child in the way he should go, and when he is old he will not turn from it.
— *The Bible*, Proverbs 22:6 (*New International Version*)

When no great harm will result, let your children do it their way, even if you know they are wrong. They will learn more from their mistakes than from their successes.
— H. Jackson Brown

Children grasp [creativity] more quickly than we do. They are more creative than grown-ups. It has not been knocked out of them.
— Emily Carr

What greater work is there than training the mind and forming the habits of the young?
— St John Chrysostom

I can never teach your children everything they need to know. But I can teach them to be curious and discontent.
— Marva Nettles Collins

Tell me, and I will forget. Show me, and I may remember. Involve me, and I will understand.

– Confucius

If you want your children to be intelligent, read them fairy tales. If you want them to be more intelligent, read them more fairy tales.

– Albert Einstein

The great teacher is not the man who supplies the most facts, but the one in whose presence we become different people.

– Ralph Waldo Emerson

You send your child to the schoolmaster, but 'tis the schoolboys who educate him.

– Ralph Waldo Emerson

By education I mean an all-round drawing out of the best in a child and man – body, mind and spirit.

– Mohandas Gandhi

The job of a teacher is to excite in the young a boundless sense of curiosity about life, so that the growing child shall come to apprehend it with an excitement tempered by awe and wonder.

– John Garrett

Anything worth learning takes time to learn, and time to teach.

– Gilbert Highet

Life is but one continual course of instruction. The hand of the parent writes on the heart of the child the first faint characters that time deepens into strength so that nothing can efface them.

— Richard Hill

The object of teaching a child is to enable him to get along without his teacher.

— Elbert Hubbard

What is learned in the cradle lasts till the grave.

— Hungarian proverb

Toddlers ask many questions, and so do schoolchildren – until about grade three. About that time, many of them have learned an unfortunate fact, that in school, it can be more important for self-protection to hide one's ignorance about a subject than to learn more about it, regardless of one's curiosity.

— Jan Hunt

A father gives his children nothing better than a good education.

— Islamic teaching

There is no such thing as a parental aide to teachers. The teacher is an aide to parents. It's the parents who rear the children.

— Jesse Jackson

Nobody ever gave you a grade for learning how
to play, how to ride a bicycle, or how to kiss. One
of the best ways to destroy love for any of these
activities would be through the use of grades, and
the coercion and judgment they represent.

– Derrick Jensen

Children are made of eyes and ears, and nothing,
however minute, escapes their microscopic
observation.

– Fanny Kemble

A child miseducated is a child lost.

– John Kennedy

At every step the child should be allowed to meet
the real experiences of life; the thorns should never
be plucked from his roses.

– Ellen Key

The loving mother teaches her child to walk alone.
She is far enough from him so that she cannot
actually support him, but she holds out her arms to
him. She imitates his movements, and if he totters,
she swiftly bends as if to seize him, so that the child
might believe he is not walking alone . . . .

– Sören Kierkegaard

How to begin to educate a child: First rule, leave
him alone. Second rule, leave him alone. Third rule,
leave him alone.

– D. H. Lawrence

The memory of having been read to is a solace
one carries through adulthood. It can wash over a
multitude of parental sins.
— Kathleen Rockwell Lawrence

Too often we give children answers to remember
rather than problems to solve.
— Roger Lewin

The important thing is not so much that every
child should be taught, as that every child should
be given the wish to learn.
— John Lubbock

Teaching a child not to step on a caterpillar is as
valuable to the child as it is to the caterpillar.
— Bradley Millar

Never help a child with a task at which he feels he
can succeed.
— Maria Montessori

The role of education is to interest children
profoundly in activities to which they will give all
their natural potential.
— Maria Montessori

There are really valid reasons why it is unwise to shield children from all violence, terror, sorrow, and death in their reading. The way to cure a child of fear of the dark is not to deny the existence of dark, but to walk with him in the dark and show him by example the restful quiet of it, and show him, too, how to avoid breaking his neck by stumbling over something he can't see.

– Robert G. Mood

What will a child learn sooner than a song?
– Alexander Pope

Don't limit a child to your own learning, for he was born in another time.

– Rabbinic saying

A child is not a vase to be filled but a fire to be lit.
– Françoise Rabelais (attributed)

I think modern educational theorists are inclined to attach too much importance to the negative virtue of not interfering with children, and too little to the positive merit of enjoying their company.

– Bertrand Russell

If you look at your child, you will see his questions before you hear them.

– Serere oral tradition

If adults but knew how much kids gather – sponge up – they would be terrorized.

– Richard Snyder

Every act of conscious learning requires the willingness to suffer an injury to one's self-esteem. That is why young children, before they are aware of their own self-importance, learn so easily; and why older persons, especially if vain or important, cannot learn at all.

– Thomas Szasz

If the places that young people go to be educated don't embody the ideals of community, cooperation, and harmony, then what young people will learn will be the behavior these institutions do exemplify: competition, hierarchy, busyness, and isolation.

– Jane Tompkins

We spend the first year of a child's life teaching it to walk and talk and the rest of its life to shut up and sit down. There's something wrong there.

– Neil deGrasse Tyson

Child: An island of curiosity surrounded by a sea of question marks.

– Unknown

I have to say, Miss Brown, that your methods are outdated and incorrect. But the children love you and are learning well. Do not on any account make any changes.

– Unknown English school inspector, about 1960

As the twig is bent the tree inclines.

– Virgil

We must believe the things we teach our children.

– Woodrow Wilson

MISCELLANEOUS

If you want to preserve knowledge and enable it to travel through time, entrust it to children.
— African saying

Can't find a dog? Why not let a child take you for a walk instead? Their owners are often happy to hand them over for a couple of hours, and the child will enjoy the novelty of being the navigator. Note: it's wise to set aside a portion of your budget to spend on child-friendly treats such as ice-creams.
— Rachael Antony and Joël Henry

Children are God's spies.
— Elizabeth Bowen

Do not pray for gold. Pray for good children, happy grandchildren.
— Chinese proverb

In God's eyes all children are beautiful but here on earth we have higher standards.
— Stephen Colbert

Babysitting is one step better than parenthood; you get paid for it and you can quit when you want.

– Debra Coppernoll

Better to be driven out from among men than to be disliked of children.

– Richard Henry Dana

Menetah, an Indonesian word, meaning: To help a little child walk by holding its hands to keep it in balance.

– Adam Jacot de Boinod, *The Meaning of Tingo – And Other Extraordinary Words from Around the World*

There was an old woman who lived in a shoe,
She had so many children she didn't know what to do;
She gave them some broth without any bread;
She whipped them all soundly and put them to bed.

– English nursery rhyme (18th century)

Children should be seen and not heard.

– English proverb

Keep me away from the wisdom which does not cry, the philosophy which does not laugh and the greatness that does not bow before children.

– Kahlil Gibran

We want our children to fit in and to stand out. We rarely address the conflict between these two goals.
– Ellen Goodman

You must write for children in the same way as you do for adults, only better.
– Maxim Gorky

When Jesus put the little child in the midst of his disciples, he did not tell the little child to become like his disciples, he told them to become like the little child.
– Ruth Bell Graham

Feel the dignity of a child. Do not feel superior to him, for you are not.
– Robert Henri

You realize that your home is as you like it when you overhear a six-year-old hostess tell a little guest, "Don't worry about making noise. Our Mommy and Daddy like children."
– Burton Hillis

Children aren't coloring books. You don't get to fill them with your favorite colors.
– Khaled Hosseini

Bricks and mortar make a house but the laughter of children make a home.
– Irish proverb

Even a bad match can beget good children.

– Jewish saying

A life-long blessing for children is to fill them with warm memories of times together. Happy memories become treasures in the heart to pull out on the tough days of adulthood.

– Charlotte Davis Kasl

Nothing you do for children is ever wasted.

– Garrison Keillor

I have a dream that my four little children will one day live in a nation where they will not be judged by the color of their skin but by the content of their characters.

– Martin Luther King, Jr.

We have kept our children so busy with "useful" and "improving" activities that we are in danger of raising a generation of young people who are terrified of silence, of being alone with their own thoughts.

– Eda J. LeShan

The car trip can draw the family together, as it was in the days before television when parents and children actually talked to each other.

– Andrew H. Malcolm

James James
Morrison Morrison
Weatherby George Dupree
Took great
Care of his Mother
Though he was only three.

– A. A. Milne

A five-year-old's definition of nursery school: A
place where they teach children who hit, not to hit,
and children who don't hit, to hit back.

– James E. Myers

When you are dealing with a child, keep all your
wits about you, and sit on the floor.

– Austin O'Malley

When I was the age of these children I could draw
like Raphael: it took me many years to learn how to
draw like these children.

– Pablo Picasso

Anyone who does anything to help a child in his
life is a hero to me.

– Fred Rogers

Keep your child's mind idle as long as you can.

– Jean Jacques Rousseau

Some of my best friends are children. In fact, all of
my best friends are children.

– J. D. Salinger

We are all children, even if most of us have forgotten it.

– Anthony Storr

Providence protects children and idiots. I know because I have tested it.

– Mark Twain

The most interesting information comes from children, for they tell all they know and then stop.

– Mark Twain

I'm not accidental. I was meant to be.

– Unknown child

In the policeman's arms
The lost child points
Towards the sweet-shop.

– Unknown Japanese writer

Children are a kind of confirmation of life, the only form of immortality that we can be sure of.

– Peter Ustinov

MOTHERS
AND MOTHERHOOD

Why should I be reasonable? I'm your mother.
— Lynne Alpern and Esther Blumenfeld

Any mother could perform the jobs of several air-traffic controllers with ease.
— Lisa Alther

A child is the apple of its mother's eyes.
— Arab proverb

Instant availability without continuous presence is probably the best role a mother can play.
— Lotte Bailyn

A mother who is really a mother is never free.
— Honoré de Balzac

I figure when my husband comes home from work, if the kids are alive, then I've done my job.
— Roseanne Barr

The God to whom little boys say their prayers has a face very much like their mother's.

— James M. Barrie

If evolution really works, how come mothers only have two hands?

— Milton Berle

Let France have good mothers and she will have good sons.

— Napoleon Bonaparte

The future destiny of a child is always the work of the mother.

— Napoleon Bonaparte

Eventually you realize that the reason God didn't always answer your prayers is that He was answering your mom's prayers.

— Robert Brault

One day someone calls her "mother." This is what she remains for the rest of her life.

— Cao Xue Qin

A mother's love for her child is like nothing else in the world. It knows no law, no pity, it dares all things and crushes down remorselessly all that stands in its path.

— Agatha Christie

The most important thing she'd learned over the years was that there was no way to be a perfect mother and a million ways to be a good one.

– Jill Churchill

What is home without a mother?

– Thomas Alva Edison

People are what their mothers made them.

– Ralph Waldo Emerson

"Mother knows best"

– Edna Ferber, title of story, 1927

A mother is not a person to lean on but a person to make leaning unnecessary.

– Dorothy Canfield Fisher

Your mother's always wrong. That's why they made her your mother.

– Bruce Jay Friedman

The mother-child relationship is paradoxical and, in a sense, tragic. It requires the most intense love on the mother's side, yet this very love must help the child grow away from the mother and to become fully independent.

– Erich Fromm

A mother does not hear the music of the dance when her children cry.

– German proverb

Mama always had a way of explaining things so I could understand them.

– Winston Groom, Forrest Gump

Have you ever heard of a son rejecting his mother because he found a nicer one?

– Ahad Ha'am

The commonest fallacy among women is that simply having children makes one a mother – which is as absurd as believing that having a piano makes one a musician.

– Sydney J. Harris

Maternal love: A miraculous substance which God multiplies as he divides it.

– Victor Hugo

The woman who creates and sustains a home, and under whose hands children grow up to be strong and pure men and women, is a creator second only to God.

– Helen Hunt Jackson

A mother never realises that her children are no longer children.

– Holbrook Jackson

Motherhood is like Albania – you can't trust the descriptions in the books, you have to go there.

– Marni Jackson

God could not be everywhere and therefore he made mothers.

> – Jewish proverb

A mother understands what a child does not say.

> – Jewish saying

There is only one beautiful child in the world and each mother has that one.

> – Latin American oral tradition

All that I am or hope to be I owe to my angel mother.

> – Abraham Lincoln

No man is poor who has had a godly mother.

> – Abraham Lincoln

I hope they are still making women like my Momma. She always told me to do the right thing, to have pride in myself and that a good name is better than money.

> – Joe Louis

That best academy, a mother's knee.

> – James Russell Lowell

When a woman has ten children there is nothing that happens in the night that she does not know about.

> – Nigerian proverb

More than in any other human relationship,
overwhelmingly more, motherhood means being
instantly interruptible, responsive, responsible.
— Tillie Olsen

Every mother is like Moses. She does not enter
the promised land. She prepares a world she will
not see.
— Pope Paul VI

The moment a child is born, the mother is also
born. She never existed before. The woman existed,
but the mother, never. A mother is something
absolutely new.
— Bhagwan Shree Rajneesh

[Motherhood] is a dead-end job. You've no sooner
learned the skills than you are redundant.
— Claire Rayner

We never make sport of religion, politics, race, or
mothers. A mother never gets hit with a custard pie.
Mothers-in-law, yes. But mothers, never.
— Mack Sennett, pioneer of slapstick movies

I may be dead but I'm still your mother.
— Nicky Silver

Let me put my finger
In your crinkled hand,
Fill me with the passion
Only mothers understand.
— Norma E. Smith

You'll see. Having a baby is like going to sleep in your own bed and waking up in Zimbabwe.
  – Sonya, unidentified mother, to her pregnant daughter

An ounce of mother is worth a pound of clergy.
  – Spanish proverb

Over the years I have learned that motherhood is much like an austere religious order, the joining of which obligates one to relinquish all claims to personal possessions.
  – Nancy Stahl

Making the decision to have a child – it's momentous. It is to decide forever to have your heart go walking around outside your body.
  – Elizabeth Stone

Mother is the name of God in the lips and hearts of little children.
  – William Makepeace Thackeray

The loveliest masterpiece of the heart of God is the heart of a mother.
  – St. Thérése of Lisieux

For the hand that rocks the cradle is the hand that rules the world.
  – William Ross Wallace

You may be used to a day that includes answering eleven phone calls, attending two meetings, and writing three reports; when you are at home with an infant, you will feel you have accomplished quite a lot if you have a shower and a sit-down meal in the same day.

– Anne C. Weisberg

Things a mother should know: how to comfort a son without exactly saying Daddy was wrong.

– Katharine Whitehorn

MOTHERS AND MOTHERHOOD

THEIR NEEDS

The distinction between children and adults, while probably useful for some purposes, is at bottom a specious one, I feel. There are only individual egos, crazy for love.

— Donald Barthelme

A sense of worthiness is a child's most important need.

— Polly Berrien Berends

Would any of you offer his son a stone when he asks for bread, or a snake when he asks for a fish?
— *The Bible*, Matthew 7:9-10 (*Revised English Bible*)

Never fear spoiling children by making them too happy. Happiness is an atmosphere in which all good affections grow.

— Thomas Bray

The toddler craves independence, but he fears desertion.

— Dorothy Corkville Briggs

The first duty to children is to make them happy.
If you have not made them so, you have wronged
them. No other good they may get can make up
for that.

— Thomas Buxton

If a child is to keep alive his inborn sense of wonder
without any such gift from the fairies, he needs the
companionship of at least one adult who can share
it, rediscovering with him the joy, excitement and
mystery of the world we live in.

— Rachel Carson

There are only two lasting bequests we can hope
to give our children. One of these is roots; the
other, wings.

— Hodding Carter

Every child needs a champion.
— Hillary Rodham Clinton

When I first became a parent, I had certain ideas
about how I was going to control the children,
and they all boiled down to this: Children just
need love.

— Bill Cosby

Two important things to teach a child: to do and
to do without.

— Marcelene Cox

THEIR NEEDS

Respect the child. Be not too much his parent.
Trespass not on his solitude.

– Ralph Waldo Emerson

People don't live long enough in Africa to worry
about cancer or the other diseases that concern us
in the Western world. In Africa the big trick is to get
to be five years old.

– David French, World Health Organization

Few parents have the courage and independence
to care more for their children's happiness than for
their "success."

– Erich Fromm

Love your children with all your hearts, love them
enough to discipline them before it is too late . . . .
Praise them for important things, even if you have
to stretch them a bit. Praise them a lot. They live on
it like bread and butter and they need it more than
bread and butter.

– Lavina Christensen Fugal

It is not giving children more that spoils them; it is
giving them more to avoid confrontation.

– John Gray

We all enter the world with fairly simple needs:
to be protected, to be nurtured, to be loved
unconditionally, and to belong.

– Louise Hart

Love, you shall perfect for me this child . . . .
> – Seamus Heaney

An infallible way to make your child miserable, is to satisfy all his demands.
> – Henry Home

The nicest thing anybody could truthfully say about me is "I love you." I would hope somebody in my family would say that truthfully to me pretty soon, like tonight.
> – Joey, aged 9 (from *Take Time to Play Checkers* by Misti Snow)

Children need models rather than critics.
> – Joseph Joubert

Children are entitled to the greatest respect.
> – Juvenal

To be a good parent, you have to put yourself second, to recognize that the child has feelings and needs separate from yours, and fulfill those needs without expecting anything in return.
> – Howard Kogan

None of us got where we are solely by pulling ourselves up by our bootstraps. We got here because somebody bent down and helped us.
> – Thurgood Marshall

To cease to be loved is for the child practically
synonymous with ceasing to live.
– Karl A. Menninger

Only the child who somewhere feels safe can take
risks. Adults are less daring than children because
they can never feel safe.
– Adam Phillips

My father had always said that there are four things
a child needs: plenty of love, nourishing food,
regular sleep, and lots of soap and water – and
after those, what he needs most is some intelligent
neglect.
– Ivy Baker Priest

The first duty of a state is to see that every child
born therein shall be well housed, clothed, fed and
educated . . . .
– John Ruskin

The child who acts unlovable is the child who most
needs to be loved.
– Cathy Rindner Tempelsman

Mankind owes to the child the best it has to give.
– U. N. Declaration of the Rights of the Child (1959)

Have you hugged your child today?
– Unknown

PARENTS
AND PARENTING

I mean, the way I see it is, one of the basic jobs
parents have is to tell you what you already know.

– Avi

The hard part of parenting is not that the task is
demanding, but that there are no guarantees.

– Craig Barnes

A perfect parent is a person with excellent child-
rearing theories and no actual children.

– Dave Barry

We never know the love of the parent until we
become parents ourselves.

– Henry Ward Beecher

Raising children is a creative endeavor, an art rather
than a science.

– Bruno Bettelheim

To bring up a child in the way he should go, travel
that way yourself once in a while.

> – Josh Billings (Henry Wheeler Shaw)

Parents don't make mistakes because they don't
care, but because they care so deeply.

> – T. Berry Brazelton

Parents are the last people on earth who ought to
have children.

> – Samuel Butler

You may be a pain in the ass, you may be bad, but
child, you belong to me.

> – Ray Charles

To understand your parents' love, bear your
own children.

> – Chinese proverb

The most difficult job in the world is not being
president. It's being a parent.

> – Bill Clinton

One of the most visible effects of a child's presence
in the household is to turn the worthy parents into
complete idiots when, without him, they would
perhaps have remained mere imbeciles.

> – Georges Courteline

If at first you don't succeed, blame your parents.

> – Marcelene Cox

Parents are often so busy with the physical rearing of children that they miss the glory of parenthood, just as the grandeur of the trees is lost when raking leaves.

– Marcelene Cox

Curlingforeldre, a word in Danish, meaning: Parents who do anything to sweep the road of life ahead of their children to ensure that it is free of obstacles.

– Adam Jacot de Boinod, *Toujours Tingo – More Extraordinary Words to Change the Way We See the World*

There are times when parenthood seems like nothing but feeding the mouth that bites you.

– Peter de Vries

Parents are just baby-sitters for God.

– C. B. Eavey

If you are a parent, recognize that it is the most important calling and rewarding challenge you have. What you do every day, what you say and how you act, will do more to shape the future of America than any other factor.

– Marian Wright Edelman

If you don't have children, the longing for them will kill you, and if you do, the worrying over them will kill you.

– Buchi Emecheta

I think when you become a parent you go from
being a star in the movie of your own life to the
supporting player in the movie of someone else's.
– Craig Ferguson

My life has been shaped by the decision two people
made over 24 years ago. They decided to adopt a
child. They got me, and I got a chance at the kind
of life all children deserve.
– Karen Fowler

To nourish children and raise them against odds is
in any time, any place, more valuable than to fix
bolts in cars or design nuclear weapons.
– Marilyn French

You don't have to deserve your mother's love. You
have to deserve your father's. He's more particular.
– Robert Frost

You are the bows from which your children as
living arrows are sent forth.
– Kahlil Gibran

Too many parents make life hard for their children
by trying, too zealously, to make it easy for them.
– Goethe

One thing I had learned from watching
chimpanzees with their infants is that having a
child should be fun.
– Jane Goodall

The beauty of "spacing" children many years apart lies in the fact that parents have time to learn the mistakes that were made with the older ones – which permits them to make exactly the opposite mistakes with the younger ones.

– Sydney J. Harris

The best combination of parents consists of a father who is gentle beneath his firmness, and a mother who is firm beneath her gentleness.

– Sydney J. Harris

The most important, relentless truth about parenthood is that "It's Not About You Any More."

– Carolyn Hax

True parenthood is self-destructive. The wise parent is one who effectively does himself out of a job as a parent. The silver cord must be broken. It must not be broken too abruptly, but it must be broken . . . . The wise parent delivers his child over to society.

– Robert Holmes

The reason parents no longer lead their children in the right direction is because the parents aren't going that way themselves.

– Kin Hubbard

The child pays, not only for the sins of the parents, but also for their mistakes and for their lack of knowledge.

– Nina Moore Jamieson

When you have your own children you will
understand your obligation to your parents.
                                        – Japanese proverb

If you are a parent it helps if you are a grown-up.
                                        – Eda J. Leshan

Having children is like having a bowling alley
installed in your brain.
                                        – Martin Mull

Children aren't happy with nothing to ignore,
And that's what parents were created for.
                                        – Ogden Nash

Oh, what a tangled web do parents weave
When they think their children are naïve.
                                        – Ogden Nash

The quickest way for a parent to get a child's
attention is to sit down and look comfortable.
                                        – Lane Olinghouse

If you bungle raising your children, I don't think
whatever else you do well matters very much.
                                        – Jacqueline Kennedy Onassis

Because of their size, parents may be difficult to
discipline properly.
                                        – P. J. O'Rourke

Two big questions present themselves to every parent in one form or another: "What kind of human being do I want my child to become?" and "How can I go about making that happen?"

— Virginia Satir

The frightening thing about heredity and environment is that parents provide both.

— Walt Schriebman

There's a time when you have to explain to your children why they're born, and it's a marvelous thing if you know the reason by then.

— Hazel Scott

Parentage is a very important profession, but no test of fitness for it is every imposed in the interest of the children.

— George Bernard Shaw

Half the world's sorrows come from the unwisdom of parents.

— Mary Slessor

The more people have studied different methods of bringing up children the more they have come to the conclusion that what good mothers and fathers instinctively feel like doing for their babies is the best after all.

— Benjamin Spock

Trust yourself. You know more [as a parent] than you think you do.

– Benjamin Spock

It's clear that most American children suffer too much mother and too little father.

– Gloria Steinem

I do not love him because he is good, but because he is my little child.

– Rabindranath Tagore

A parent should never make distinctions between his children.

– *The Talmud*

Parenthood remains the greatest single preserve of the amateur.

– Alvin Toffler

Children are harder to raise than in the past, and every generation of parents thinks so.

– Unknown

Parents forgive their children least readily for the faults they themselves instilled in them.

– Marie von Ebner-Eschenbach

Parents of young children should realize that few people, and maybe no one, will find their children as enchanting as they do.

– Barbara Walters

I cannot exaggerate the importance of parental harmony. The welfare of the children rests more on parental unity than on any child-rearing expertise the parents may have.

— John White

The hardest part of raising children is teaching them to ride bicycles. A father can run beside the bicycle or stand yelling directions while the child falls. A shaky child on a bicycle for the first time needs both support and freedom. The realization that this is what the child will always need can hit hard.

— Sloan Wilson

The thing that impresses me most about America is the way parents obey their children.

— The Duke of Windsor

To the faults of his children, everyone is blind.

— Yiddish saying

Children can forgive their parents for being wrong, but weakness sends them elsewhere for strength.

— Leontine Young

PLAY AND LEISURE

Every age wants its playthings.
— American proverb

The average four-year-old laughs or smiles 400 times each day; the typical adult laughs or smiles fifteen times each day. Clearly we have much to learn about playfulness from children.
— Roland S. Barth

You can do anything with children if you only play with them.
— Otto von Bismarck

Babies are the ones who always get all the cool toys. I never get anything.
— Blake, aged 5, quoted in *Parenting for Dummies*

Never go near a kid who's holding a water hose unless you want to get wet.
— H. Jackson Brown

Play catch with a kid.
— H. Jackson Brown

The work will wait while you show the child the rainbow, but the rainbow won't wait while you do the work.

– Patricia Clafford

The essence of childhood, of course, is play, which my friends and I did endlessly on streets that we reluctantly shared with traffic.

– Bill Cosby

Our culture has made leisure an industry but knows very little about play.

– Margaret Cowley

If play is to be genuine it must be lighthearted and pursued without purpose. That is why we usually fail if we try to have fun.

– Larry Dossey

It is a happy talent to know how to play.

– Ralph Waldo Emerson

Lambs skip and bound, kittens and puppies seem wild with the joy of life; and little children naturally run, leap, dance and shout in the exuberance of that capacity for happiness which the young human heart feels as instinctively as the flower buds open to the sun. To repress their natural joyousness, not to direct and train it for the good, seems to be the object of most parents.

– Sarah Josepha Hale

The business of being a child interests a child not at all. Children very rarely play at being other children.

– David Holloway

Play is one of the main bases of civilization.

– Johan Huizinga

For a small child, there is no division between playing and learning; between the things he or she does "just for fun" and the things that are "educational." The child learns while living and any part of living that is also educational is also play.

– Penelope Leach

Were I a philosopher, I should write a philosophy of toys, showing that nothing else in life need to be taken seriously, and that Christmas Day in the company of children is one of the few occasions on which men become entirely alive.

– Robert Lynd

Children: Of all people, the most imaginative. They abandon themselves without reserve to every illusion.

– Thomas Macaulay

Only where children gather is there any real chance of fun.

– Mignon McLaughlin

Children will watch anything, and when a broadcaster uses crime and violence and other shoddy devices to monopolize a child's attention it's worse than taking candy from a baby. It is taking precious time from the process of growing up.

– Newton Minow

It is to be noted that children's plays are not sports, and should be regarded as their most serious actions.

– Montaigne

Playing at make-believe, the young child becomes the all-powerful person he cannot be in reality. In pretending, the child takes control of his otherwise powerless position.

– Joanne E. Oppenheim

In our play we reveal what kind of people we are.

– Ovid

Child with spinning top. Every time he throws it, it lands at the very center of the world.

– Octavio Paz

To every job that must be done, there is an element of fun. Find the fun and, snap, the job's a game.

– Mary Poppins (Bill Walsh and Don DaGradi, screenwriters)

Children do not play ordinary conventional games unless they are encouraged to do so by the older boys and girls. Children's "games," strictly speaking, are not games at all. They are the child's inmost reality. They are the child's life-illusion. They turn back to them with a sigh of relief from the impertinent intrusive activities of grown up people.

– J. C. Powys

One way to think about play is as the process of finding new combinations of known things – combinations that may yield new forms of expression, new inventions, new discoveries, and new solutions.

– Fred Rogers

You are worried about seeing him spend his early years in doing nothing. What! Is it nothing to be happy? Nothing to skip, play, and run around all day long? Never in his life will he be so busy again.

– Jean Jacques Rousseau

I had another amusement which I much enjoyed. On a Sunday, when the park was crowded, I would climb to the very top of a large beech tree on the edge of our grounds. There I would hang upside down and scream and watch the crowd gravely discussing how a rescue should be effected. When I saw them reaching a decision I would get the right way up and quietly come down.

– Bertrand Russell

By engaging in play, children more or less deliberately "try on" selves to be and worlds to be in. This is because the only way a child can "have" a self is by trying one on.

– Tamar Schapiro

You've made your bed; now, go bounce on it.

– Peter Scott

We don't stop playing because we grow old; we grow old because we stop playing.

– Herbert Spencer (also attributed to George Bernard Shaw)

A child loves his play, not because it's easy, but because it's hard.

– Benjamin Spock

A man is as young as he feels after playing with children.

– Unknown

During my childhood I created imaginary playmates. Then one night they stole all my toys.

– Unknown

Play: Joy unrefined.

– Unknown

The child had every toy his father wanted.

– Robert Whitten

THEIR POTENTIAL

In every child who is born, under no matter what circumstances, and of no matter what parents, the potentiality of the human race is born again.

— James Agee

I think parents should forget the genius bit – what you want is a human being, a mensch, not a genius.

— Jerome Bruner

Our children are not going to be just "our children" – they are going to be other people's husbands and wives and the parents of our grandchildren.

— Mary S. Calderone

All kids are gifted; some just open their packages earlier than others.

— Michael Carr

There is no finer investment for any community than putting milk into babies.

— Winston Churchill

The greatest gift you can give your child is the freedom to actualize his unique potential self.
— Fitzhugh Dodson

If you want to see what children can do, you must stop giving them things.
— Norman Douglas

We must teach our children to dream with their eyes open.
— Harry Edwards

A few days after we came home from the hospital, I sent a letter to a friend, including a photo of my son and some first impressions of fatherhood. He responded, simply, 'Everything is possible again.' It was the perfect thing to write because that was exactly how it felt.
— Jonathan Safran Foer

THEIR POTENTIAL

Children are what you make them.
— French proverb

If we are to reach real peace in this world . . . we shall have to begin with the children.
— Mohandas Gandhi

If children grew up according to early indications, we should have nothing but geniuses.
— Goethe

In praising or loving a child, we love and praise not that which is, but that which we hope for.
— Goethe

No one has yet fully realized the wealth of
sympathy, kindness and generosity hidden in the
soul of a child. The effort of every true education
should be to unlock that treasure.

– Emma Goldman

Children are our most valuable natural resource.

– Herbert Hoover

A child is born in part, he is made in part, and in
part he makes himself.

– H. H. Horne

Children are apt to live up to what you believe
of them.

– Lady Bird Johnson

Be nice to your children. They may grow up
to be writers.

– Katerina Stoykova Klemer

All children are artists, and it is an indictment
of our culture that so many of them lose their
creativity, their unfettered imaginations, as they
grow older.

– Madeline L'Engle

In the baby lies the future of the world. The mother
must hold him close so that he will know the world
is his. The father must take him to the highest hill
so he can see what his world is like.

– Mayan saying

When I approach a child, he inspires in me two sentiments; tenderness for what he is, and respect for what he may become.

– Louis Pasteur

Every child is an artist. The problem is how to remain an artist once he grows up.

– Pablo Picasso

Don't forget that compared to a grownup person, every baby is a genius. Think of the capacity to learn! The freshness, the temperament, the will of a baby a few months old!

– May Sarten

Let our children grow tall, and some taller than others if they have it in them to do so.

– Margaret Thatcher

Children may be 20 percent of the population but they are 100 percent of the future.

– David Tyack

Children are the only future of any people.

– Frances Cress Welsing

Children are the living messages we send to a time we will not see.

– John W. Whitehead

PRIORITIES

A sparkling house is a fine thing if the children aren't robbed of their luster in keeping it that way.
— Marcelene Cox

Lack of time . . . might be the most pervasive enemy the healthy family has.
— Dolores Curran

We are willing to spend the least amount of money to keep a kid at home, more to put him in a foster home, and the most to institutionalize him.
— Marian Wright Edelman

Each of us will have our own different ways of expressing love and care for the family. But unless that is a high priority, we will find that we may gain the whole world and lose our own children.
— Michael Green

Your children need your presence more than your presents.
— Jesse Jackson

If you want your children to turn out well, spend twice as much time with them as you think you should and half the amount of money.
— Esther Selsdon (also attributed to others)

Could I climb to the highest place in Athens, I would lift my voice and proclaim, "Fellow Citizens, why do you turn and scrape every stone to gather wealth and take so little care of your children to whom one day you must relinquish it all?"
— Socrates

As a political culture, we are pretty cool with cutting preschool programs for the most vulnerable people in the country, but we are outraged – spurred to bold, decisive, instant action – by inconvenience in air travel.
— Shawn Vestal

It's a little frustrating sometimes when you listen to your children saying their prayers. It costs thousands and thousands of dollars to raises them and you get mentioned ahead of the goldfish but after the gerbil.
— Pat Williams and Ken Hussar

THEIR QUALITIES

Children's talent to endure stems from their ignorance of alternatives.

– Maya Angelou

I see the mind of the five-year-old as a volcano with two vents: destructiveness and creativeness.

– Sylvia Ashton-Warner

The law of grab is the primary law of infancy.

– Antoinette Brown Blackwell

Children think not of what is past, nor what is to come, but enjoy the present time, which few of us do.

– Jean de La Bruyère

There is a deep wisdom inaccessible to the wise and prudent but disclosed to babes.

– Christopher Bryant

When will we teach our children in school what they are? We should say to each of them: Do you know what you are? You are a marvel . . . . And when you grow up, can you then harm another who is, like you, a marvel?

– Pablo Casals

Children usually know the truth before we tell them.

– Alan Cohen

From children you must expect childish acts.

– Danish proverb

Bunget, a word in the Manobo language, in the Philippines, meaning: As a child, to want something one can't have, get angry, and then refuse it when it is finally offered.

– Adam Jacot de Boinod, *Toujours Tingo – More Extraordinary Words to Change the Way We See the World*

A world without children is a world without newness, regeneration, color and vigor.

– James Dobson

[A child] is Nature's fresh picture newly drawn in oil, which time, and much handling, dims and defaces. His soul is yet a white paper unscribbled with observations of the world, wherewith at length it becomes a blurred notebook.

– John Earle (1623)

Children and fools speak the truth.

> – English proverb

When children stand quiet they have done some ill.

> – English proverb (17th century)

The children of other nations always seem precocious.

> – F. Scott Fitzgerald

Child: An ever-bubbling fountain in the world of humanity.

> – Friedrich Froebel

His name is Marcus: he is four and a half and possesses that deep gravity and seriousness that only small children and mountain gorillas have ever been able to master.

> – Neil Gaiman

Unlike grownups, children have little need to deceive themselves.

> – Goethe

Children have more energy after a hard day of play than they do after a good night's sleep.

> – Gumperson's Law

Pretty much all the truth telling there is in the world is done by children.

> – Oliver Wendell Holmes, Sr.

No one ever keeps a secret so well as a child.

– Victor Hugo

Children are remarkable for their intelligence and ardor, for their curiosity, their intolerance of shams, the clarity and ruthlessness of their vision.

– Aldous Huxley

There's nothing more contagious than the laughter of young children; it doesn't even have to matter what they're laughing about.

– Criss Jami

Children are the true connoisseurs. What's precious to them has no price – only value.

– Bel Kaufman

One of the reasons children are such duds socially is that they say things like, "When do you think you're going to be dead, Grandma?"

– Jean Kerr

The fundamental job of a toddler is to rule the universe.

– Lawrence Kutner

Credulity is the man's weakness but the child's strength.

– Charles Lamb

THEIR QUALITIES

A child is a person who can't understand why
someone would give away a perfectly good kitten.
– Doug Larson

Children ask better questions than do adults.
"May I have a cookie?" "Why is the sky blue?"
and "What does a cow say?" are far more likely
to elicit a cheerful response than "Where's your
manuscript?" "Why haven't you called?" and
"Who's your lawyer?"
– Fran Lebowitz

Even when freshly washed and relieved of all
obvious confections, children tend to be sticky.
– Fran Lebowitz

Notoriously insensitive to subtle shifts in mood,
children will persist in discussing the color of a
recently sighted cement mixer long after one's own
interest in the topic has waned.
– Fran Lebowitz

Children are travelers newly arrived in a strange
country of which they know nothing.
– John Locke

Children know the grace of God
Better than most of us. They see the world
The way the morning brings it back to them,
New and born and fresh and wonderful.
– Archibald MacLeish

Children see magic because they look for it.
— Christopher Moore

Who knows the thoughts of a child?
— Nora Perry

Nature makes boys and girls lovely to look upon so
they can be tolerated until they acquire some sense.
— William Lyon Phelps

Behold the child, by nature's kindly law,
Pleased with a rattle, tickled with a straw.
— Alexander Pope

Children . . . laugh easily and heartily: they have
nothing to lose and hope for little. In renunciation
lies a delicious taste of simplicity and deep peace.
— Matthieu Ricard

Children . . . have no use for psychology. They
detest sociology. They still believe in God, the
family, angels, devils, witches, goblins, logic, clarity,
punctuation, and other such obsolete stuff . . . .
When a book is boring, they yawn openly. They
don't expect their writer to redeem humanity, but
leave to adults such childish illusions.
— Isaac Bashevis Singer

Children today are tyrants. They contradict
their parents, gobble their food, and tyrannize
their teachers.
— Socrates (5th century BC), probably apocryphal

THEIR QUALITIES

Kids: they dance before they learn there is anything that isn't music.

– William Stafford

She announced her age right away, for children consider their ages every bit as important as their names.

– Trenton Lee Stewart

Children share with geniuses an open, inquiring, uninhibited quality of mind.

– Chauncey Guy Suits

Know you what it is to be a child? . . . . It is to believe in love, to believe in loveliness, to believe in belief; it is to be so little that the elves can reach to whisper in your ear; it is to turn pumpkins into coaches and mice into horses, lowness into loftiness, and nothing into everything, for each child has its fairy godmother in its soul.

– Francis Thompson

Children have but little charity for one another's defects.

– Mark Twain

A characteristic of the normal child is he doesn't act that way very often.

– Unknown

Some day science may be able to explain why a child can't walk around a mud puddle.

– Unknown

No symphony orchestra ever played music like a two-year-old girl laughing with a puppy.

– Bern Williams

SIBLINGS

When brothers agree, no fortress is so strong as their common life.

– Antisthenes (5th-4th century BC)

– Antisthenes (5th-4th century BC)

How good and pleasant it is when brothers live together in unity!

– *The Bible*, Psalm 133:1 (*New International Version*)

An advantage of having only one child is that you always know who did it.

– Erma Bombeck

It is difficult to anticipate bringing home an invader of the love affair that one has created with the first child.

– T. Berry Brazelton

Comparison is a death knell to sibling harmony.

– Elizabeth Fishel

Having one child makes you a parent; having two you are a referee.

– David Frost

In form and feature, face and limb,
I grew so like my brother
That folks got taking me for him,
And each for one another.

– Henry Sambrooke Leigh

Children of the same mother do not always agree.
– Nigerian proverb

Where there's a sibling,
There's quibbling.

– Selma Raskin

Big sisters are the crabgrass on the lawn of life.
– Cartoonist Charles Schulz's character Charlie Brown

He ain't heavy . . . . He's my brother.
– Song by Bobby Scott and Bob Russell

More than Santa Claus, your sister knows when
you've been bad and good.

– Linda Sunshine

Your sister is the only creature on earth who shares
your heritage, history, environment, DNA, bone
structure, and contempt for stupid Aunt Gertie.

– Linda Sunshine

['T]is a shameful sight,
When children of one family
Fall out, and chide, and fight.

– Isaac Watts

Ss

SLEEP

Wo-mba, a word in the Bakweri language, in Cameroon, meaning: The smiling in sleep by children.

– Adam Jacot de Boinod, *Toujours Tingo – More Extraordinary Words to Change the Way We See the World*

A sleeping child gives me the impression of a traveler in a very far country.

– Ralph Waldo Emerson

There never was a child so lovely but his mother was glad to get asleep.

– Ralph Waldo Emerson

After you've done all your preparation, tuck them into bed, kiss them goodnight, turn on the night light, *and leave*. It's that simple.

– Sandra Hardin Gookin

Honey, the baby woke up, it's your turn to get him.
Honey? I know you're not asleep, I can tell by the
way you're breathing.

– Sandra Hardin Gookin

It is not advisable to put your head around your
child's door to see if it is asleep. It was.

– Faith Hines

Sleep, baby, sleep!
Thy father's watching the sheep,
Thy mother's shaking the dreamland tree,
And down drops a little dream for thee.
Sleep, baby, sleep.

– Elizabeth Prentiss, Cradle Song (1887)

Blessings on him that first invented sleep.

– Spanish proverb

Now I lay me down to sleep,
I pray the Lord my soul to keep.
If I should die before I wake,
I pray the Lord my soul to take.

– The New-England Primer (1735)

Rock-a-bye, baby, in the tree top
When the wind blows the cradle will rock
When the bough breaks the cradle will fall
Down will come baby, cradle and all

Baby is drowsing, cosy and fair
Mother sits near in her rocking chair
Forward and back, the cradle she swings
Though baby sleeps, he hears what she sings

Rock-a-bye baby, do not you fear
Never mind, baby, mother is near
Wee little fingers, eyes are shut tight
Now sound asleep until morning light
            – Traditional lullaby (various versions exist, the first
                  appearing in *Mother Goose's Melody* in 1765)

We learn from experience. No man ever wakes his
baby a second time just to see it smile.

– Unknown

THEIR UNIQUENESS

The average child is an almost non-existent myth. To be normal one must be peculiar in some way or another.

– Heywood Broun

Nine sons she bore, nine separate characters.

– Chinese proverb

Children in a family are like flowers in a bouquet: there's always one determined to face in an opposite direction from the way the arranger desires.

– Marcelene Cox

Every child is different and handles punishment differently. You can't always apply the same punishment to every child.

– Shirley Hardin

Allow children to be happy in their own way, for what better way will they ever find?

– Samuel Johnson

THEIR
VULNERABILITIES

The child's sob in the silence curses deeper than the strong man in his wrath.

– Elizabeth Barrett Browning

Children can stand vast amounts of sternness. They rather expect to be wrong and are quite used to being punished. It is injustice, inequity and inconsistency that kill them.

– Robert Capon

The child's grief throbs against its little heart as heavily as the man's sorrow; and the one finds as much delight in his kite or drum as the other in striking the springs of enterprise or soaring on the wings of fame.

– E. H. Chapin

Better to cheat an old gray head than to trick a small child.

– Chinese proverb

To neglect children is to murder them.

– Daniel Defoe

It is a cowardly abuse of power to ill-treat a child.

– La Comtesse de Ségur

In the little world in which children have their existence . . . there is nothing so finely perceived and so finely felt, as injustice.

– Charles Dickens

Woe to the man who offends a small child!

– Fyodor Dostoevsky

So long as little children are allowed to suffer, there is no true love in this world.

– Isadora Duncan

If we don't stand up for children, then we don't stand for much.

– Marian Wright Edelman

It is a spiritually impoverished nation that permits infants and children to be the poorest Americans.

– Marian Wright Edelman

A cruel or rude child is a ghastly thing, but a cruel or brutal parent can do infinitely more harm.

– Christopher Hitchens

THEIR VULNERABILITIES

Young children scare easily – a tough tone,
a sharp reprimand, an exasperated glance, a
peeved scowl will do it. Little signs of rejections –
you don't have to hit young children to hurt them
– cut very deeply.

– James L. Hymes

All children are potential victims, dependant on the
world's goodwill.

– Sally Kempton

I'd like to have more power . . . . I do have power but
since I'm small, everyone takes it away from me.

– Kristin, aged 10 (from Take Time
to Play Checkers by Misti Snow)

He had grown up in a country run by politicians
who sent the pilots to man the bombers to kill the
babies to make the world safer for children to grow
up in.

– Ursula K. Le Guin

A torn jacket is soon mended, but hard words bruise
the heart of a child.

– Henry Wadsworth Longfellow

Why is it that a child's death amounts to a tragedy,
but the death of millions is merely a statistic?

– Patrick McDonald

THEIR VULNERABILITIES

The children are always the chief victims of
social chaos.

— Agnes Meyer

A child's tears rend the heavens.

— Nokhem Shtutshkof

The fundamental condition of childhood is
powerlessness.

— Jane Smiley

A child, punished by selfish parents, does not feel
anger. It goes to its little private corner to weep.

— Rose Tremain

Of all of mankind's inequities, injustice to young
children is the most despicable.

— Francois Truffaut

It is a shameful thing to insult a child. It has its
feelings. It has its small dignity, and since it cannot
defend them, it is surely an ignoble act to injure
them.

— Mark Twain

THEIR VULNERABILITIES

Never call your kid a name like dumb or any other unkind comment about how they act. I say this because once in a while it happens to me. When it does happen to me, my mom or dad usually say they are sorry, but even if they do, it still hurts me for a while inside.

– Unknown ten-year-old girl (from *Take Time to Play Checkers* by Misti Snow)

Did you know that the worldwide food shortage that threatens up to five hundred million children could be alleviated at the cost of only one day, only *one* day, of modern warfare.

– Peter Ustinov

INDEX

Battista, O. A. – **Fathers and Fatherhood**
Baxter, Geraldine – **Humor**
Beck, Allen – **Boys and Girls**
Beecher, Henry Ward – **Parents and Parenting**
Belloc, Hillaire – **Boys and Girls**
Benchley, Robert – **Humor**
Berends, Polly Berrien – **Beginnings; Needs**
Berger, Thomas – **Humor**
Berle, Milton – **Grandparents; Mothers and Motherhood**
Betjeman, John – **Childhood**
Bettelheim, Bruno – **Childhood; Example and Influence;**
    Parents and Parenting
The Bible – **Blessings; Faith; Fathers and Fatherhood; Learning;**
    Needs; Siblings
Bigelow, Hilda – **Fathers and Fatherhood**
Billings Josh (Henry Wheeler Shaw) – **Parents and Parenting**
Bismarck, Otto von – **Play and Leisure**
Blackwell, Antoinette Brown – **Qualities**
Blake, Bessie – **Discipline**
Blumenfeld, Esther – **Mothers and Motherhood**
Bombeck, Erma – **Humor; Siblings**
Bonaparte, Napoleon – **Mothers and Motherhood**
Boulanger, Nadia – **Discipline**
Bowen, Elizabeth – **Miscellaneous**
Bowring, John – **Families**
Boyle, Peter – **Fathers and Fatherhood**
Bradshaw, John – **Example and Influence**
Brault, Robert – **Mothers and Motherhood**
Bray, Thomas – **Needs**
Brazelton, T. Berry – **Discipline; Grandparents;**
    Parents and Parenting; Siblings
Brever, Billy – **Humor**
Briggs, Dorothy Corkville – **Needs**
Brittain, Vera – **Beginnings; Blessings**
Broun, Heywood – **Beginnings;Uniqueness**
Brown, Charlie *See* Schulz, Charles
Brown, H. Jackson – **Children and Grown-Ups; Discipline;**
    Learning; Play and Leisure
Browning, Elizabeth Barrett – **Vulnerabilities**
Bruner, Jerome – **Potential**
Brussell, Eugene E. – **Boys and Girls**
Bruyère, Jean de la – **Qualities**
Bryant, Christopher – **Qualities**
Buarque, Cristovam – **Community**
Burke, Edmund – **Example and Influence**
Burke, Leo J. – **Beginnings**
Burney, Fanny – **Childhood**

Butler, Samuel – **Parents and Parenting**
Buxton, Thomas – **Needs**

Earle, John – **Qualities**
Eavey, C. B. – **Parents and Parenting**
Edelman, Marian Wright – **Parents and Parenting; Priorities; Vulnerabilities**
Edison, Thomas Alva – **Mothers and Motherhood**
Edwards, Harry – **Potential**
Egyptian proverb – **Blessings**
Einstein, Albert – **Learning**
Eixhter, Jean Paul – **Fathers and Fatherhood**
Elium, Don – **Discipline**
Elium, Jeanne – **Discipline**
Elkind, David – **Childhood**
Ellerbee, Linda – **Fathers and Fatherhood**
Emecheta, Buchi – **Parents and Parenting**
Emerson, Ralph Waldo – **Beginnings; Blessings; Learning; Mothers and Motherhood; Needs; Play and Leisure; Sleep**
English nursery rhyme – **Boys and Girls; Miscellaneous**
English proverb – **Blessings; Boys and Girls; Miscellaneous; Qualities**
Euripides – **Fathers and Fatherhood**

Faber, Frederick W. – **Fathers and Fatherhood**
Ferber, Edna – **Mothers and Motherhood**
Ferguson, Craig – **Parents and Parenting**
Fishel, Elizabeth – **Siblings**
Fisher, Dorothy Canfield – **Mothers and Motherhood**
Fitzgerald, F. Scott – **Qualities**
Foer, Jonathan Safran – **Potential**
Forbes, Malcolm – **Growing Up**
Fowler, Karen – **Parents and Parenting**
Frakes, Dennis – **Discipline**
French proverb – **Beginnings; Fathers and Fatherhood; Food and Drink; Potential**
French, David – **Needs**
French, Marilyn – **Parents and Parenting**
Freud, Sigmund – **Fathers and Fatherhood**
Friedman, Bruce Jay – **Mothers and Motherhood**
Froebel, Friedrich – **Qualities**
Fromm, Erich – **Mothers and Motherhood; Needs**
Frost, David – **Siblings**

Frost, Robert – **Parents and Parenting**
Fugal, Lavina Christensen – **Needs**
Fulghum, Robert – **Example and Influence**
Fuller, Margaret – **Blessings**

Gaiman, Neil – **Qualities**
Gandhi, Mohandas – **Children and Grown-Ups; Learning; Potential**
Garrett, John – **Learning**
Geisel, Theodore – **Growing Up**
King George V of England – **Fathers and Fatherhood**
German proverb – **Food and Drink; Mothers and Motherhood**
Gibran, Kahlil – **Miscellaneous; Parents and Parenting**
Ginott Haim – **Example and Influence**
Goethe – **Parents and Parenting; Potential; Qualities**
Goldman, Emma – **Potential**
Goodall. Jane – **Parents and Parenting**
Goodman, Ellen – **Fathers and Fatherhood; Miscellaneous**
Gookin, Sandra Hardin – **Sleep**
Gorky, Maxim – **Miscellaneous**
Graham, Ruth Bell – **Miscellaneous**
Gray, John – **Needs**
Gray, Patsy – **Grandparents**
Green, Michael – **Priorities**
Groom, Winston – **Mothers and Motherhood**
Guliani, Rudolph – **Grandparents**
Gumperson's Law – **Qualities**

Ha'am, Ahad – **Mothers and Motherhood**
Hale, Sarah Josepha – **Play and Leisure**
Haley, Alex – **Grandparents**
Hardin, Shirley – **Uniqueness**
Hardin, Virgil – **Discipline**
Harris, Sydney J. – **Mothers and Motherhood; Parents and Parenting**
Hart, Louise – **Needs**
Hax, Carolyn – **Parents and Parenting**
Hayes, Helen – **Childhood**

Ii

Jj

INDEX

Kk

L

Mm

INDEX

Pp

Praed, Winthrop – **Childhood**
Prentiss, Elizabeth – **Sleep**
Priest, Ivy Baker – **Needs**
Putney, Mary Jo – **Childhood**

Qq

Quindlen, Anna — **Beginnings; Growing Up**

Rr

Rabbinic saying – **Learning**
Rabelais, Françoise – **Learning**
Rachel Carson– **Needs**
Rajneesh, Bhagwan Shree – **Mothers and Motherhood**
Raskin, Selma – **Siblings**
Rayner, Claire – **Mothers and Motherhood**
Ricard, Matthieu – **Qualities**
Richardson, Frank – **Humor**
Lord Rochester – **Humor**
Rogers, Fred – **Discipline; Miscellaneous; Play and Leisure**
Roosevelt, Eleanor – **Fathers and Fatherhood**
Rousseau, Jean Jacques – **Childhood; Families; Miscellaneous;
    Play and Leisure**
Rudner, Rita – **Grandparents**
Runbeck, Margaret Lee – **Childhood**
Ruskin, John – **Blessings; Needs**
Russell, Bertrand – **Childhood; Learning; Play and Leisure**
Russell, Bob – **Siblings**

Ss

Salinger, J. D. – **Miscellaneous**
Salk, Lee – **Fathers and Fatherhood; Food and Drink**
Samalin, Nancy – **Discipline**
Sandburg, Carl – **Beginnings**
Santayana, George – **Families**
Sapirstein, Milton – **Families**
Sarten, May – **Potential**
Satir, Virginia – **Parents and Parenting**
Scalia, Antonin – **Families**

Uu

Vv

Ww

150

ABOUT THE COMPILER

You've Made Your Bed, Now Go Bounce On It is Gordon Jackson's seventh anthology of quotations. Orginally from South Africa, he has taught journalism and worked in academic adminstration at Whitworth University, in Spokane, Wash., since 1983.

He completed his undergraduate work at the University of Cape Town. He also has an MA from Wheaton College and a doctorate in mass communication from Indiana University. He worked as a journalist in Johannesburg in the 1970s.

Jackson is married to another South African, Sue, who he says helps keep his accent honest. They have two adult children, Sarah and Matthew.